PASSPORT
TO THE CORNER OFFICE

KEYWORD SEARCH

For quick access to the Corporate Resource Guide, use the following keywords:

TIPPING GUIDE: tip1

INTERVIEW TIPS: interview1

FORMAL DINING DIAGRAM: dining1

www.writtenindetroit.com

Twitter: @WriteDetroit
Facebook: WrittenInDetroit

PASSPORT
TO THE CORNER OFFICE

The Starter's Guide to Corporate Life

R.J. KING

King Publishing Co.

www.rjkingpublishing.com
www.writtenindetroit.com
www.momentumbooks.com
www.dbusiness.com

First Edition
Printed in the United States

Cover image courtesy of The Stanislav Orekhov Studio, Moscow.
www.d-e-s-i-g-n.ru
Place Setting image by Stephanie King, *skingillustration@gmail.com*.

THIS BOOK IS DEDICATED TO:

My Parents
John and Barbara

My Brothers and Sisters (and their Spouses)
Kathy, Linda (Scott), Nancy (Craig), Patrick (Linda), Mary (Brad),
Suzy, Maureen (Marc), and John (Li-Hsing)

My Nieces and Nephews
Mary Clare, Maureen Megan, Rosemary, Zachary, James, Kathryn,
Christopher, Nicholas, Stephanie, Crystal, Michael, Melissa,
Matthew, Megan, Amanda, Joshua, Julien, Sophie, Kate, and Ian

Thank to the following families/firms:

Farbman	Jackson	Silverman
Huvaere	Bassett	Sakwa
Rimanelli	Powell	Shayota
Venegas	DiDio	Celani
Lustig	Wong	Vicari
Barnhart	Steward	Wolk
Carmona	Moran	Young
Davis	Harrington	Sweis
Babiarz	Schneider	Huth Lynett
Bieri	Karmanos	Brooks Kushman
DiChiera	Snethkamp	Conway MacKenzie

And Special Thanks to the Team:
Josef Bastian (Author)
Cassidy Zobl (Designer)
Anne Berry Daugherty (Copy Editor)
Carl Winans (Web Designer)

INTRODUCTION

One stumble in the corporate world can cost you dearly. Avoid an apology, show up your boss, or embarrass a client and you can kiss that multimillion-dollar business deal goodbye. And that's just the social side.

In the corporate world, if you strive to lead 175,000 employees to record-breaking profits or have just staked a tech company in your parents' garage, help yourself by mastering corporate culture, capital markets, technology, regulations, and myriad design, engineering, manufacturing, and sales activities.

It's equally important to recognize that strong management skills are a prerequisite for anyone starting or striving to lead a foundation, a charitable group, a political campaign, or a major civic endeavor.

Let's face it: Change is inevitable. One day you're working on the Chicago Mercantile Exchange, the next year you're opening a food processing plant in Bolivia, and, 20 years later, you're CEO of an Italian fashion house. And when you retire, you'll be asked to chair a symphony, a zoological society, or a fine art museum.

This book details the facets of what a newly hired person should know about global business, and helps prepare anyone for the corporate world — including high school, college, and graduate students. What's more, it offers educational and social guidance for young professionals, parents of young children, cultural groups, and anyone looking to enhance a business, an organization, or a career.

As I reflect on 20 years of meeting, interviewing, and writing about entrepreneurs, executives, doctors, lawyers, retailers, athletes, entertainers, and administrators, I wish I had a resource like this when I was 17 years old.

I wish I had known early on how to read people quickly, how to avoid the wannabes, the pretenders, and the people who want their ring kissed, and how to surround myself with gifted, passionate, and visionary people.

I wish I had known that the secret to life is to add value.

It's what this book is all about.

Let me know if I can add more.

— R.J. King

rjking@rjkingpublishing.com

CONTENTS

CONTENTS

CHAPTER ONE

GETTING STARTED

"IF I CAN'T DELIVER EXCELLENCE, IT'S NOT WORTH DOING."
— **SID FORBES**, SENIOR PARTNER, FORBES CO.

Whether you're in high school, college, or graduate school, everyone wants their first corporate job to include a six-figure salary, a corner office, a luxury sedan, a generous expense account, a smart phone/tablet/iMac, membership at a country club, and four weeks of vacation (on top of two weeks of holidays).

But it rarely happens that way.

Most people toil all of their life — 60 years or longer — and never reach the executive suite.

Look around ... it's true.

Just 27 percent of Americans earn a four-year college degree, 9 percent have a master's degree, and 3 percent hold a Ph.D., according to the U.S. Census Bureau and various surveys. At the same time, more and more jobs require a college degree.

Consider what happened to the workers who built typewriters. When typewriters gave way to computers, the workers on the typewriter assembly line had to find another job that paid $10 an hour. Given the increasing sophistication of shipping and logistics, the computer industry established much of its labor operations overseas.

Today, the majority of computer jobs in the United States are in management, research and development, design, sales, distribution, and marketing — almost all of which require a college or a graduate degree.

Assuming a 40-hour week, a $10-an-hour job in a factory or at a retail store works out to $20,800 a year, or $400 a week, which may or may not include benefits like health care insurance or a matching 401(k) plan.

When you factor in federal, state, and local taxes — which typically represent 29 percent of a person's annual income — it can be tough to make ends meet.

On the other hand, the average salary of a college graduate with a business degree is $51,541 (2012), according to the National Association of Colleges and Employers — which works out to $991 per week before taxes.

Now, consider the average median salary of a chief executive officer, or CEO. The task of overseeing a major corporation is worth $730,000 a year, according to *salary.com*. That's $14,038 a week before taxes.

Over 60 years, consider what each job generates in gross income:

- **Assembly Line Worker:** $1.2 million
- **Average College Graduate:** $3.1 million
- **Average CEO:** $43.8 million

So how do you become a CEO?

Try a college degree, hard work, luck, and determination.

But the better question is ...

Can you handle the corner office?

Running a major corporation that employs thousands of people is incredibly time-consuming, often thankless, and filled with pitfalls.

If you oversee a public company, things can change rapidly. A board of directors will show you the exit door if there's a sudden drop in the share price.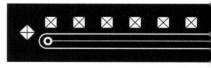

And there are forces beyond your control. What happens when assembly line workers in China who are building your smart phones are committing suicide by jumping off the factory roofs? How will you react? What will you tell their families?

What's more, you could face criminal charges because you failed to foster and monitor a safe working environment.

On the other hand ...

One of the best lessons from corporate life is to avoid the consumption of power. Don't get caught up in the trappings of the office. If you're more concerned with the thread count of your custom suits than the working environment of your employees, the problems will come soon enough.

Bad karma begets bad karma.

Think long and hard about whether the CEO position is right for you. I have plenty of friends who have started great companies, built them up to 300 or so employees, and then sold the enterprise (or a major chunk of it).

They move on. They start over. They want new challenges.

Administrative duties were gobbling up their creative time. Every new employee took them further and further away from exploring new spaces or taking a great technology to market.

It's easy when you're starting by yourself; the hard part is scaling up a great idea. As your product or service takes off, more and more of your time will be devoted to meeting or exceeding the following:

- Revenue must outpace spending (that's where the profits come in)
- Operations
- Daily and weekly meetings with key managers
- Monthly meetings with investors (or as needed)
- Constant oversight of key suppliers
- Constant oversight of all competitors
- Time management (including your social life)
- Hiring and firing
- Talent raids
- Advertising, marketing, public relations, sponsorships
- Employees (and their benefit packages)
- Government regulations
- Ever-changing interpretations of government regulations
- Lawyers
- Politicians
- Security breeches
- Accidents
- Media attacks

And that's just to name a few.

If you dream about running a major corporation, remember it's just a dream. Before you sit in the CEO's chair and experience all of the forces that go into running an organization with thousands of employees spread across the world, take the time to prepare. Enroll in as many classes as possible, whether in accounting, engineering, business management, government relations, social media, public speaking, or design. Learn a second or a third language.

Maximize your versatility.

There is no guarantee you'll reach the CEO's chair, or even the executive suite. If you do, be indispensable. If the company you work at undergoes a management shake-up, you'll either be promoted or take on more duties (hopefully with an increase in salary).

But nothing is set in stone. In mid-2012, General Electric, one of the largest and most successful corporations in the world, dismissed dozens of managers in its mammoth energy department. The company split the division into three parts: Power and Water, Oil and Gas, and Energy Management. GE CEO Jeff Immelt saw an opportunity to save up to $300 million in overhead costs by removing a management layer. Under the new plan, the CEOs appointed to run the three divisions now report directly to Immelt.

What happened to all of the executives who thought their jobs were secure? After all, GE routinely posted strong earnings. Some of the managers were re-assigned, but the rest had to find new work or retire. For those searching for another job, the process was that much easier because they had experience, a college degree, and marketable skill sets.

For those managers who chose retirement, the options included a part-time job, a volunteer position, spending quality time with grandchildren, or returning to campus to teach.

Others may have decided to start a business.

As long as people add value and continue to reach for their dreams, life has purpose.

Whether you join a great company or start your own, the pressure to perform can be grueling. I've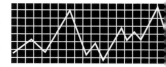
seen friends get the top job. It's great, at first, when you visit their new office. But you'll find, as I did, that the office becomes all-consuming. There's no avoiding the tasks of keeping nervous investors happy, overseeing thousands of workers, monitoring competitors, streamlining operations, and anticipating regulations (that, hopefully, your team of lobbyists helped write).

What makes more sense in the grand scheme of things is to find a niche where you can add value free of most outside forces. Since you will spend the next 60 or so years of your life working, make sure your career path aligns with your passions.

If you want to serve great food and earn more than $100,000 a year waiting tables in a five-star restaurant, go for it. But it won't be a cakewalk.

You must stay current on nutrition, slow-cooking, organic sourcing, and wine trends. If you don't, your customers will soon lose interest. The same discipline applies to anyone striving to own a great restaurant (a sit-down restaurant lasts six years, on average).

What keeps people coming back?

Great food and great service, yes, but it's also the experience. As a waiter or restaurant owner, what news can you share about the weather patterns in the northern region of Chile that vastly improved the 2007 Cabernet Sauvignon?

Working with the kitchen staff, what new dish can you create from locally sourced walleye complete with a roux-based sauce, butter-whipped parsnips, and sweet corn?

Stay current. Be ready to reassure your clientele that the off-Broadway play they're about to see is a winner, despite the particularly nasty review in *The New York Times*.

Almost anyone can wait on a table.

To set yourself apart, learn how the kitchen works, how to cook seasonally, where the ingredients are sourced, and which wines pair best with a dish like Coq Au Vin.

To stay ahead, read articles inside and outside of your field. Every day I read *The Wall Street Journal*, *The New York Times*, the *Financial Times*, and our two local papers, *The Detroit News* and the *Detroit Free Press* (online). I also read about 50 magazines a month, including *Fast Company*, *Forbes*, *Fortune*, *Bloomberg Businessweek*, *GQ*, *The New Yorker*, *Men's Health*, *Time*, and *Wired*.

Every weekday morning, there's the leading business news radio show. There's also national news or business programs on TV or cable. At night, there are educational shows, or anything to take your mind off things for an hour or so.

If you want to work in Apple's research labs, aspire to be the best.

Use your time in Cupertino, California, well.

SURVIVAL RATE OF NEW BUSINESSES:

70%
LAST **2 YEARS**

50%
LAST **5 YEARS**

33%
LAST **10 YEARS**

25%
LAST **15 YEARS (OR MORE)**

To stay ahead, you must read trade journals, tinker in your spare time, attend conferences inside and outside of your field, stay active online, circulate, set trends, hang with the cool kids, and learn what's coming.

Most of all, work hard. Nothing creates progress faster than hard work.

Take it a step further.

Develop a product or service that no one knows they need. Or anticipate trends and capitalize on them. Better yet, set the trends yourself.

As luxury mall owner Sid Forbes says: "I always wanted to be the best I could be. If I can't deliver excellence, it's not worth doing."

He's right. No one remembers the average. The last thing you want your parents, teacher, or boss to say was that you are an average person.

When it's time for your funeral, will people say you lived an average life? Will your tombstone read: AVERAGE?

Your funeral should be a celebration of your life. Emanuel Steward, the famous boxing manager who trained 41 world champion fighters throughout his career — including Hilmer Kenty, Lennox Lewis, Thomas Hearns, Oscar De La Hoya, and Julio Cesar Chavez — had more than 1,000 people at his funeral in October 2012. The service, held at Greater Grace Temple in Detroit, included a moving song by Aretha Franklin, and many world-champion boxers flew in and made remarks.

Steward, 68, touched the lives of hundreds of people. In the lead-up to the 1984 Summer Olympics, Steward and Muhammad Ali took what was a very average U.S. boxing team and molded the competitors into a formidable force. The pair trained the boxers in a private location and paid for many of their expenses. The result was amazing: 9 Gold, 1 Silver, and 1 Bronze medal. The performance set a record that still stands.

One secret Steward shared toward the end of his career: People should live a great life with the tools they are given.

In other words, you have to stand out … even if you have average skills.

How do you overcome average? Add value.

At home, perhaps one of your childhood chores was to cut the lawn. A great job, to be sure, given it provides immediate gratification. But if you don't mow in straight lines, neglect to trim the edges, or leave clippings all over the sidewalk, why bother?

As a general rule, when you visit someone's home for the first time, check out the landscaping. If the outside of the house looks good, chances are there are lots of good things happening inside.

I have a routine when visiting a company for the first time. I check the exterior landscaping and then head indoors. Is the office tidy and neat, or are there stacks of paper and old office equipment strewn here and there?

Make a point of visiting the bathroom. Is it well-appointed or sloppy? If there are issues here, it usually means the office or home environment needs work. In one instance, I visited a small research laboratory and found the lone bathroom had a shelf above the toilet where they made the coffee. God only knows where they kept the cream.

For people who visit your office or your home, roll out the red carpet.

Act like you're an ambassador hosting an embassy reception. Be mindful of everyone in the room. Are your guests engaged, or do they require assistance? Act as if nothing can upset you. Watch how your parents, family members, and successful friends act.

Do your best at every job presented. Frequency and excellence go hand in hand. Will there be failures? Sure.

School and life are about finding and improving upon your strengths and overcoming your weaknesses. No one is perfect. Not everyone can be the quarterback, or the cheerleader, or the valedictorian, or the next Steve Jobs.

It's the same in the business world. Not everyone can be the CEO, the lead designer, a board member, or the president of the United States.

So what's the point?

It's all about how you look at things.

You could go through school and get a degree. Nice job.

But it's better to go through school and learn everything you can. Use the school to your advantage. Start your own company and use the school's facilities. Meet in the study room, the cafeteria, or out in the parking lot. Jump on the computers, or tap into the library. You have free time; use the school's assets to your advantage.

You can register a company online, typically for a $50 fee from a city or state.

Chances are your school is paid for, you're working your way through, or you've taken out substantial loans to fund your education.

No matter.

Use the school to advance your interests.

Your education is being paid for, one way or another.

Don't let them use you.

Try every school offering on for size as a measure of discovering your future career(s). That's why there are so many subjects covered beginning in kindergarten, and on through grade school, high school, and college.

The best advice is to stay in school, get the best grades you can, and graduate. No one can ever take a degree away from you.

Once you're working, remember that change is constant. Industries, companies, organizations, and government structures evolve every day — whether up, down, left, right, or sideways.

Have a backup career plan or two. Apart from my writing and editing, I have a real estate sales license in escrow. I attend six hours of continuing education each year to stay current. If I ever need it, it's there. Many people work two jobs, or have hobbies at home that earn them extra money.

As you select your major(s), make sure it's something you like to do, and there is strong demand for your skills. You don't want to earn a four-year degree and find out your occupation is flooded with candidates. Specialize in two or three fields to improve your marketability.

Another reason to stay in school is the growing sophistication of the global economy. As lower-skilled jobs head overseas, they are being replaced by higher-skilled jobs in the United States and other developed countries. The shift in the economy has impacted nearly everything and will continue to do so for several more decades. People with a strong work ethic and a postsecondary degree can go a long way.

More and more, factory robots are becoming the norm. For students who pursue a degree in robotics engineering, there are plenty of job openings that pay more than $100,000 a year. What's more, you can land a job in nearly any advanced or developing country of your choosing.

Consider, also, that a good majority of the 14 million jobs to be created in the United States by 2022 will most likely require a degree from a community college, a university, or a graduate school, according to the Boston Consulting Group. A postsecondary diploma is a valuable tool as you go through life.

Stay active. It's another secret to life.

Take the advice of Nancy M. Schlichting, CEO of Henry Ford Health System in Detroit, and use all of your vacation time. As she says, work is stressful enough, so carve out time each day for family and friends.

Travel the world. Explore new cultures. Find out what makes each culture tick. Right now, exports account for 14 percent of the nation's GDP (gross domestic product), according to the U.S. Commerce Department, so chances are good that international travel will be a part of your job.

I've worked and vacationed in Paris, Torino, Shanghai, and La Paz, as well as nearly every state in America. I spent a week at an economic camp at the former headquarters of the Marconi Wireless Telegraph Co. north of San Francisco, drove a Hummer 1,000 miles from Tijuana down the Baja California peninsula, had lunch with the captains of the Italian automotive industry in a glass atrium atop Fiat's former world headquarters in Torino, played golf at Shanghai Links (a Jack Nicklaus-designed course set on the shores of the Pacific Ocean), and swam with the dolphins at the Dolphin Research Center in Grassy Key, Florida.

Wherever you go, leave your mark.

You may have a soft voice, which isn't an asset when you're asked to address the General Assembly of the United Nations.

So speak up.

Hold the microphone close and project your voice. Practice at home. Musical acts like U2, The Beatles, No Doubt, and Santana got their start playing in small, obscure clubs. The crowds were generally rough and rowdy, with no record producer in sight.

To get ahead, they met the right people, at the right time. Some of it was luck — but a lot of their future success came from understanding basic business principles, along with networking. They met the right people who provided the necessary financial backing and recording space. When successful artists aren't networking, they're honing their craft. They continue to master new genres, instruments, and horizons.

As you go through life, you will be asked to address a large group at some point. The farther the microphone is from your mouth, the less likely the people in the back will hear you.

And you want to be heard.

Hold the microphone close. If you're at a podium, be sure to adjust the microphone. Take the time to get it right. If you have a remote mic, hold it close and give it all you've got. Ask if everyone can hear you at the start. Command the room.

You may not be the best speaker, presenter, or debater, but people will remember you if they can hear what you have to say. If debate is something you enjoy, perhaps you have a future in politics.

If not, move on.

But leave a mark. Learn from the experience.

Throughout your life, think of nearly everything as a target at an archery range. Nike, for example, seeks out the coolest kids to learn what they're listening to, wearing, and buying. Of all the kids out there, they're looking for the trendsetters, who will help them anticipate design trends. The coolest kids are in the center of the target. Nike goes to great lengths to identify and discern what the trendy kids are wearing, sharing, and pairing.

Your goal is to be in the center of your field. If you're starting a law career and seek to specialize in environmental issues, figure out how to get to the center of the target — and stay there.

How do you do that?

First, ask around at school or the office to see who the best lawyers are. Next up is research. Look for local business magazines, newspapers, or law journals that rate the performance of environmental lawyers. Perhaps you want to specialize in soil remediation or water runoff. What classes or conferences can you sign up for that will expand your knowledge base?

Once you know the identities of the best environmental lawyers, spend a semester or two as an intern at the respective law firms. Alternatively, you may want to take an internship in a related field, perhaps with a judge or a prosecutor.

In turn, meet and spend time with government officials in your chosen field. You may want to work at a government job for a few years to learn what makes, say, the local EPA office tick. Nearly every region has someone working in the public sector in an area that pertains to your chosen field.

In addition, there are local associations that represent the legal industry, such as the state bar, a defense society, or a law foundation. Make it a point to join as many of these organizations as possible. If you're representing a chemical conglomerate, imagine how grateful the company will be if you heard through a former EPA colleague that the federal agency was planning to regulate your client's production lines.

By getting a jump on the information, and working with the corporation's lobbying team, you may be able to eliminate or streamline the regulations, which often come with an inspection fee. Only Congress can raise taxes, so that's why the EPA and other government operations charge a fee for services rendered (they often want the money upfront).

Your local Congressional representatives can be of great assistance in the matter, as well. Learn and get to know the local, state, national, and international government leaders who represent your industry or clients. 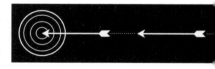 Once again, network with as many people as possible.

It works for any endeavor.

If you want to develop shopping malls full of the finest stores and restaurants, circulate within the respective professional fields.

Try the local chapter of the American Institute of Architects, or the state chapter of the International Council of Shopping Centers. If you do anything in the real estate, retail, or restaurant field, you will want to circulate within these groups.

Pay the dues, attend the meetings, go to the conferences, and volunteer to be on a committee or two. Soak up as much knowledge as possible.

Once you learn the ropes of the local association, move up to the national and international level. It's a great way to expand your knowledge base, add value to your profession, and improve the likelihood that your firm will be successful.

It's the same for robotics, urban farming, health care, or private security.

Get to know and circulate with key people in your industry. Join a business advisory group like the Young Presidents' Organization (YPO), Entrepreneurs' Organization (EO), or Vistage International. Once you've been selected for membership, learn from your colleagues, help solve their problems, and volunteer to make the group larger by boosting membership.

Keep in touch with your professors and instructors. They could come in handy with a corporate problem you're facing years down the road. Whatever your profession, find out who the best researchers are in your field and partner with them.

You never know where it will take you, what you will learn, or how it can help advance your career. Remember, nothing happens overnight. It can take years to reach the top of your profession, be accepted into a national or international organization, or receive an invitation to a White House dinner.

But if you work hard, stay humble, and march forward every day, the good things in life will come your way.

2 LISTEN AND LEARN

DON'T BE AFRAID TO ASK QUESTIONS. NO ONE KNOWS EVERYTHING. IF YOU DON'T ASK, THE ANSWER WILL ALWAYS BE "NO."

Consider the career path of Norm Nickin, a private security expert who protected Frank Sinatra, one of the great singers and entertainers of the 20th century. Frank was a private man, but his fame was such that he typically had to book the entire floor of a hotel while on tour. Security, even in the 1970s, was a necessary precaution.

Nickin, president of National Security Service in Birmingham, Michigan, was hired to prevent well-meaning fans from monopolizing Frank's private life. Nickin was brilliant at listening and learning.

Because Nickin was a smart guy, he kept his eyes and ears open and tried to add value wherever he could.

Nickin and his team didn't leave anything to chance. They worked with the hotel to prevent the elevators from stopping on the floor where Frank was staying (typically the penthouse level). The stairway doors were locked. A special phone was set up and the number was only shared with Frank's family and close friends.

As Nickin and his team gained Frank's trust, they would stay after their shifts and gather in Frank's room to watch a baseball game. Frank loved to watch baseball.

As time went on, Frank's inner circle was his security team. He relied on Nickin to make sure that every hotel on tour had excellent TV reception (few parts of the country were wired for cable in the 1970s). Nickin also made sure the room was stocked with Frank's favorite liquors and snacks. Frank surrounded himself with the best — and he gave back.

When Frank's friends would ask about security, Frank recommended Nickin and his team.

Soon, Nickin got to know Sammy Davis Jr., a wonderful entertainer who performed on stage in Las Vegas, toured, produced albums, and appeared in movies like *Ocean's 11*, the original 1960 film starring Sammy, Frank, Peter Lawford, Dean Martin, and Joey Bishop.

One thing Nickin noticed about Sammy was that he kept his jewelry — gold watches, bracelets, necklaces, and cuff links — in a satin handkerchief. He simply didn't trust the hotel safe. In those days, few rooms had safes, so the only option was the main safe behind the registration desk.

A forgetful person, Sammy would hide his jewelry under the bed, in a drawer, or inside a bathroom vanity. When Nickin traveled with Sammy, he always made sure the entertainer had his jewelry before the limousine pulled out into traffic. When Nickin wasn't around, he would alert hotel security so Sammy didn't leave without his jewelry.

It was a great system, and Sammy was the first to tout Nickin's work when anyone asked. As a result of the great reviews he received, Nickin now runs a very successful private security firm, and a great deal of his company's growth was due to the connections he made.

Nickin is also caring, astute, honest, reliable, and trustworthy. He never puts himself in front of his clients. And he always looks two or three steps ahead.

It goes back to the archery target. Frank and Sammy were in the center of the entertainment world. Nickin moved in and out of the center of that circle — and, because of it, he was at the center of his profession.

Always try to stay in the center of the circle, both in your own career and that of others.

There are only so many people who can operate in the center of a given industry or profession. You may be one ring out from someone else's center, but as long as you have access to people who move through that particular focal point, you're in good shape.

If you are two or more rings from the center, it poses a challenge. It means you have to network more, raise your knowledge base, and work harder.

Some people don't want to strive for the center. That's fine. As long as it's not laziness or apathy that are holding you back, there's nothing wrong with being in the outer ring. Perhaps you're raising a family and working part time. Be the best parent you can be. Attend PTA meetings, volunteer to oversee a scout troop, or hold bake sales to raise money for new playground equipment.

Don't, however, sit around all day on Facebook or Twitter. Get out and meet people. Be the center of your own ring. You want people to come to you for advice. You also must seek out the best advice possible.

Don't be afraid to ask questions. No one knows everything. If you don't ask, the answer will always be "No."

Why ask questions? Consider the following ...

In the United States, Nickin and his team are incredibly adept at providing security and working with local, state, and federal authorities. The reason: America has a system of laws and regulations that nearly everyone respects, and the judicial system is accountable and protective of those laws and regulations (passed by duly elected lawmakers).

The American people don't always elect the smartest people. That's why there are elections every two, four, and six years. It provides for a changing of the guard before things get too far out of hand. The old saying that "absolute power corrupts absolutely" is certainly relevant in any country.

By protecting its citizens from the ravages of absolute power, America is a bright beacon. But, around the world, the right of freedom is not universally respected. Most English-speaking countries are safe to travel within — but that's not always the case.

In Third World countries, you can't leave anything to chance. If you're planning to develop a business relationship in a Third World country, it's best to bring in experts like Nickin and ask a lot of questions.

Traveling to and from a Third World nation could be a catastrophe waiting to happen.

Imagine if your private jet is seized at the main airport in Abuja, Nigeria.

The military has surrounded your plane, forcibly removed all of the passengers and crew, and has started interrogating everyone on the tarmac.

Is now a good time to offer a bribe?

Perhaps the local police captain has a beef with your company. The military may not even be involved. It could be a private army overseen by a warlord who views the manufacturing plant you're planning as an affront to his authority.

More than likely he feels personally threatened. He is accustomed to absolute rule. The U.S. government may be of limited assistance in cases like this. Unless it's a kidnapping, they likely won't get involved.

Your company, meanwhile, may not be of much assistance, either. In some corporations, a married executive with a family will receive better treatment in a Third World crisis such as a kidnapping than an unmarried executive. The reason is twofold: A family typically holds more insurance than an individual, and a family is a bigger public relations nightmare than an individual.

A wife with two crying children pleading on TV for a husband's return presents a major problem for even the most crass of company managers. If they don't do everything possible to expedite the safe return of the executive, other managers within the company will jump ship to more socially conscious corporations. What's more, if the company sells consumer products, the negative publicity will impact sales.

Before you start working for a company with international reach, be sure to research past grievances. More importantly, how were those grievances resolved? If the company has a history of problems in foreign countries, especially Third World countries where the rule of law is controlled by one or many warlords, think long and hard about whether that company is right for you.

If you plan to work at a U.S. embassy in a hostile country, you will be a very big target.

You could be kidnapped, shot, or killed outside of the embassy gates.

Inside, you are relatively safe, but rogue entities like al-Qaida have no qualms about setting off a car bomb nearby.

Fear is the controlling force of any two-bit despot or wannabe regime. Ruling by fear allows terrorist leaders to substantiate their power and solidify their base with what is often a poor and largely uneducated population.

In other words, ignorance is bliss for a terrorist regime looking to fill the minds of the surrounding populace with misinformation, lies, and the threat of retribution. If you don't toe the line, they'll use a rope to hang you.

Is there honor among thieves? Yes and no. If you plan to conduct business in a country like Nigeria, where corruption is prevalent, be prepared to hire your own team, including top-notch security. But before you do, make sure the upside is greater than the downside. Perhaps you plan to build a power plant that research shows will vastly improve the quality of life in Nigeria.

It's a worthy — and, presumably, a profitable — cause.

But the Nigerian government likely won't agree. They can stonewall you from the very beginning with bribes, regulations, or threats. The reason: If citizens get access to cheap power, they can afford more things like computers with Internet service. Once the citizens learn of the livelihood offered in reputable countries, they'll want to replicate it at home or move to a better place. That worries even the most barbaric warlord.

On the other hand, a Third World government could defy all of the negative stereotypes and allow you to proceed with the energy plant.

Great, right? Not really.

After your company invests millions of dollars to open the plant, the government could seize it. The reason why doesn't matter; the fact is, the plant has been taken over by the military.

You may have a signed contract, but that won't matter. If a foreign leader decides to seize your company's factories, offices, or infrastructure, there's not much you can do about it in the short term.

Consider what happened in April 2012 when Argentina's political leadership, in full concert with its Congress, nationalized the YPF unit of Repsol S.A., a Spanish energy company. Argentina's government seized oil and natural gas wells inside its borders, along with exploration equipment and leased land. The government acted on the grounds that Repsol did not invest enough in oil and natural gas production.

That's a problem for Argentina, given it defaulted in 2002 on a massive amount of debt. As a result, the country found it difficult to raise money in the global capital markets. It had to spend limited currency assets on fuel imports to meet demand.

Repsol was caught in the middle.

Instead of dealing with the core problems of its debt, Argentina's leadership seized Repsol's energy assets. The move had the added benefit of raising the government's standing with a citizenry tired of power outages and high energy costs.

Argentina needs a reboot. The powers that be grabbed control of YPF's assets to boost the supply of oil and natural gas and, in doing so, they gained points on the streets.

The future consequences of the decision, however, are left to twist in the wind.

BUSINESS TRAVEL IN THE THIRD WORLD:

SHARE TRAVEL PLANS WITH **KEY STAFF ONLY**

SET MEETINGS **AFTER ARRIVAL**

USE **LOCAL** CURRENCY

PHOTO-COPY PASSPORT

NEVER VENTURE OUT AT NIGHT ALONE

Consider Repsol is fighting the takeover in the world courts, and has filed grievances against the state takeover. A government panel in Argentina is weighing how to compensate the company, but the decision could take years to conclude.

Then there's the problem of collecting on the compensation. It's not like the country can write a check for $10 billion, which is what Repsol initially wanted for its controlling stake in YPF.

There are long-term considerations, as well. What happens with the oil rigs, gas-generation plants, and drilling equipment? The equipment must be maintained, repaired, and eventually replaced.

Do you think Repsol will do it? Not likely, due to the dispute.

Other companies could be approached, but while replacement equipment can easily be bought, who will install it?

Repsol pulled out its key engineers and technical people, and there isn't a ready supply of replacement labor willing to go in and maintain the system. Given what happened with Repsol, any new entity will want the money up front.

Again, Argentina's leadership pushed its problems down the road, where they often get worse.

Argentina is not a country that will attract a great deal of foreign investment today, which further undermines its ability to pay down debt. In one swift move, the country went from a second-class country to a Third World nation in the eyes of the global capital markets.

All the Nickins in the world aren't going to fix the problems in places like Argentina. If you install and build major capital equipment in a corrupt country, be cognizant of the fact that the assets could be taken over without notice.

If you're shipping consumer goods to and from a struggling country and a shady cast of government leaders appropriates the goods, the monetary damage might not be as acute. Still, the operation must be shut down to limit more losses.

If a despot seizes your workers, be prepared to get them out. It may take U.S. military intervention or a private army. Whatever you do, it's going to be expensive. The best advice is to do your homework before you invest in a foreign land. And be sure to ask a lot of questions.

3 IT'S A BUSINESS WORLD

YOUR EDUCATION DOESN'T STOP JUST BECAUSE YOU GRADUATED FROM COLLEGE.

There are four basic groups in corporate life: business, nonprofit, government, and unions. The best can network within all four groups, but it isn't easy. So many organizations, so many players, and each marching to a single or shared agenda. You'll never keep everyone happy, and you will kill yourself trying.

It takes years before key players will trust you, information can be obtained readily, and you have the green light to bring other trusted people into the center of a given circle.

When that happens, congratulations are in order; you've made it! But the journey never ends. There are many more groups and industries to meet and learn from.

There's global trade, logistics, courts of law, academia, chambers of commerce, trade associations, cultural organizations, conservancies, charitable endeavors, regulators ...

For everyone you meet, get a business card and build your database. And be sure to offer your card. If you're in high school or college, have business cards prepared with your name, school, projected graduation date, planned degree(s), and your e-mail address (school e-mail is better than your personal e-mail).

I made up my first business cards right before graduating from high school. It was straightforward — nice paper stock with my name, phone number, and college (the University of Michigan–Dearborn). I had no e-mail address because the Internet wasn't up and running at that time.

Those business cards helped me land my second internship and my first real job. My first internship was with the Wayne County Juvenile Court; my second internship was with the chief justice of the Michigan Supreme Court, G. Mennen Williams. From there, I landed a job as a file clerk with the legal department at General Motors' world headquarters. My supervisor remarked it was the first time she had ever seen a business card from a student. I worked full time at GM during the summer, and two days a week during the school year. I also worked part time as a short-order cook at a Jewish delicatessen.

Buy a nice business card holder. You don't want to hand over a card that is wrinkled or dirty.

If you give someone your card and they don't give you one back, consider it poor form on their part. Ask for their card. If the person doesn't have one, ask them to send you their contact information. You also can enter their information in your smart phone or jot it down on a piece of paper (you can use the back of your business card). Add it to your database. If someone fails to send you their contact information, they likely have too much going on, or not enough.

When you receive a business card, read it right away. You never know whom you are meeting. It could be a CEO or a person who works in your career field — a research scientist, a marketing director, or a heart specialist.

Follow up with a quick e-mail. Keep it short and simple. The first sentence should recap your meeting, and mention the name of the event or occasion. In the next sentence, get to the point. Is there a call to action, such as a follow-up meeting or a job interview? That's it. If you're too wordy, the other person may hit the delete button.

Be sure to bring your business cards everywhere and have a backup stash in your car, backpack, attaché case, or locker.

When you're meeting someone for the first time, be sure to listen intently. Allow other people to be heard. Build your knowledge base. If the person is boring, endure things for a while and move on. Never be rude. Thank everyone for his or her time.

Yes, there are people who are incredibly busy, so don't be afraid to be direct. Extend an invitation to contact you if they ever need a favor. Hopefully they'll do the same if the occasion arises.

For high-level people like Bill Ford, chairman of Ford Motor Co., or Dan Akerson, chairman and CEO of General Motors Co., know what subjects interest them.

Be prepared before you make your introduction. Don't dwell on your favorite things; focus on their interests. You want to encourage feedback.

Ford is a dedicated environmentalist and a strong advocate for managing global gridlock through technology integration. In 2050, roughly 70 percent of the world's population of 9.2 billion people will be living in urban areas. If the streets are so crammed with vehicles, how will public safety agencies reach an emergency such as a fire, shooting, explosion, or riot? It's the same for food deliveries and other daily needs.

Ask Ford what he's working on to reduce global gridlock. He loves talking about it, and he needs to get the message out. Learn from him. Perhaps your company can help him?

Akerson graduated from the U.S. Naval Academy and is a big proponent of discipline, given his background. Ask him about his days with the Navy, and what he's doing today to help with fundraising or mentorships. Perhaps you can offer assistance. If you can, Akerson will never forget it.

But be sure what you offer is with the right intention. Don't have ulterior motives.

When you meet someone for the first time, be inquisitive. People love to talk about themselves. I've been in plenty of conversations where all the other person knows is my name, my title, and perhaps the name of our magazine. Let the other person talk. Your education doesn't stop just because you graduated from college. Be sure to exchange business cards and follow up with a hand-written message or e-mail. It's the right thing to do, and it could pay dividends down the road.

CHINESE COLOR GUIDE:

RED REPRESENTS GOOD FORTUNE

BLACK IS ASSOCIATED WITH HEAVEN

GREEN IS FOR WELLNESS/ HARMONY

BLUE RELATES TO IMMORTALITY

WHITE SYMBOLIZES DEATH

High-level people like Ford and Akerson don't typically carry business cards, especially on the home front. For one thing, most everyone knows them. Secondly, they simply don't have the time to meet and follow up with everyone; it's not possible when they have 125,000 employees spread all over the world.

So how do you stay in touch? Get to know their chief of staff or lead public relations person. If you can develop a good working relationship, they will provide the easiest path to the CEO or chairman.

When you're networking and don't know anyone, introduce yourself and say where you are from. Put the other person on a pedestal. Ask what they do, where they were raised, and where they were schooled. Armed with such data, it's amazing how quickly you can put the pieces together to see where a person stands on any number of issues.

Did your new acquaintance grow up in a city, a suburb, or on a farm? Do they have brothers and sisters, or are they an only child? Are their parents still together, or did they split up? Did your new friend attend a major university, or a smaller college?

If you know the person you just met was raised on a farm, was an only child, and his or her parents are still together, chances are very good that you're dealing with a stable, confident person who may be lacking a few social graces. It's likely they didn't spend much time eating at nice restaurants or attending an opera or a Bach recital.

Knowing this, you can easily predict your new friend is environmentally conscious, works well alone, and is open to learning new things. The reason is they spent most of their childhood and adolescence on a farm, so outside of school and chores, they learned to entertain themselves. They likely read a great deal. They will stand by their convictions. They know hard work is rewarding. They know how to plant a garden and contribute to its success.

On the other hand, they may be somewhat naïve, find networking a challenge, and appear reclusive. If they have talent, help them build their database.

After you've worked in the corporate world long enough, the challenge of meeting new people and contacts comes easy. But managing all of that data can be a chore, if not done properly.

So how do you manage your contacts? Use keywords. Every time I meet a talented photographer, for example, I make sure to list the word "photographer" next to the person's name on my iPhone. A couple of years might go by, and while I might forget the photographer's name, I can easily search my phone.

Don't forget to use keywords for your contacts. I often exchange business cards but, at times, there's something missing. In one instance, after exchanging business cards with a pleasant lady, I saw that her card denoted that she worked as a broker at a residential real estate company with no mention that she was the president of the Philippine American Chamber of Commerce, which is how she introduced herself.

Without missing a beat, I took my pen (always carry a nice writing instrument) and jotted the information on her card. With many other people to meet at a given event, it pays to write things down. You can't remember every conversation, so don't try. If you don't have a pen, or the card is too glossy to write on, enter a note on your phone calendar for the next day. Or send yourself an e-mail or text. That way, it's easy to follow up.

I meet 20 or 30 new people in an average week. I take a little time each Sunday to update my contacts. If I need help one day understanding Philippine culture, having that one contact pop up quickly makes all the difference in the world.

Always be courteous.

Don't be the person who extends an offer of assistance, and then never provides it. People will be impressed that you care enough to reconnect, and even more impressed when you follow through.

What happens if someone presses their case at a public event? For me, some people aren't shy about wanting to be featured in the magazine — whether for a resource list such as Top Lawyers, party pictures, columns, in-depth profiles, you name it.

One night at a black-tie reception, an artist all but demanded that I review her book. As a rule, we don't review books, but she was adamant that we should make an exception since her book had been mentioned in national magazines.

It wasn't a business book, so that was out. I suggested we get together for coffee and explore whether there was an article about her journey since the book was launched. In hindsight, it was the right move. But personalities can be hard to predict, especially for people who are ambitious.

It was interesting. Every time someone walked by and said hello, she was on her best behavior. But as soon as we were alone (as much as you can be alone in the center of a cocktail party), she raised her voice and was direct.

I put her e-mail in my phone (she didn't have a card) and promised to follow through. It turned out to be one of the best columns I've written. Did she make things uncomfortable? Yes. But she had passion, and she made it work. For myself, I kept an open mind.

Whenever you're in a situation where someone is pressing you in public, diffuse the tension as quickly as possible. Of course, be cordial. Take down their information, or ask for a business card, and be sure to follow through.

Life in the corporate bubble can be harsh. There are times when people may choose to spread lies about you for their own personal gain. They want your job and will do just about anything to get it.

This happened at *The Detroit News* from time to time. As a business writer who broke hundreds of stories, I was a target. A few times, I suspect the competition called and pretended to be a person who was misquoted in an article. After getting hauled into my editor's office, my response was to call the person who was really quoted. Most often, I had my editor make the call while I stood there and listened on the speakerphone. Never once did the person on the other line say they were misquoted. What's more, they said they never called to complain.

Since I was doing my job correctly, these accusations never amounted to anything. The lesson here is to be ready to defend your actions at a moment's notice. As you make important decisions at your job, always ask yourself how others will perceive your actions.

Consider another incident at the paper: A public company in Michigan became the takeover target of a larger rival from another state. I was smack dab in the middle. The battle went on for months, and the stakes were high for both sides. Had the takeover been successful, numerous people would have lost their jobs. When two companies become one, you don't need two chief financial officers (CFOs), two human resource managers, or two receptionists.

Most often, the company that gets taken over loses out. When it comes time to make a decision over which CFO to keep, the management team driving the takeover will look to keep their team intact. They don't want to upset the apple cart and fire their own people, as those who stay will become uneasy and begin contemplating a new job with a more loyal company. Loyalty is a powerful force in the corporate world, and it could mean the difference in keeping your job or losing it.

The lesson here is that mergers and acquisitions happen every day. Keep that in the back of your mind as you arrive at work each day. Are you striving to be the best executive, engineer, or design director on the planet? If not, there's someone out there ready to take your job.

As for the merger battle, I suspect the company looking to acquire the firm here in Michigan made accusations about my relationship with the takeover target. There was never anything beyond a professional relationship. From time to time, I would see the family at a charitable event, and while we made small conversation (I always ask how a person's business is doing, and what's coming down the road), that was it.

Obviously, someone was spreading rumors. I got hauled into my editor's office and was asked point-blank whether I had accepted cash from the family or flown on their plane. No and no. I've had people offer me cash to write a glowing story about them, but I always turned them down. As soon as people offer cash in exchange for a good story, I cut them off permanently — but in a nice way. No sense making an enemy.

As much as I encourage cordial relations with everyone, there are times when you must draw a line in the sand and make your stand. It could be that someone on your team isn't performing, a competitor takes a cheap shot, or a politician doesn't like the fact that your company is downsizing in his or her district.

At times, the decisions you make will affect hundreds of lives. If you have to let 300 people go because a particular division is underperforming or global competition is undercutting your profits, you have to make the cuts.

It's a tough predicament for anyone. But just remember, someone has to do it. The company can't operate on autopilot; it takes humans to run and monitor the operations. If you think about it, a company is a perfect organization on paper. It's humans that screw things up.

At the magazine, I use the same philosophy. The magazine is perfect, and it's our staff — including myself — that makes the mistakes. Steadfastly, through countless readings among several people (including an outside copy editor), we catch every mistake by the time the pages are printed. But every so often, one slips through. It keeps you humble.

Don't worry if you occasionally screw up early on in corporate life. You're still learning. As long as the mistakes are due to inexperience or circumstances beyond your control, things will be fine. But if you're lazy, strong-headed to the point of upsetting your team, or a tyrant, things will eventually fall apart for you.

No one knows everything. That's why networking is so important. If you get caught in the corporate bubble for too long, you lose perspective. Treat everyone the same, whether it's a CEO, an assembly line worker, a farmhand, a store clerk, or a politician.

Recall the basic corporate groups — business, nonprofit, government, and unions. Learn to mingle within all four groups with relative ease. At times, you'll need to reach deep within each group to tackle a given challenge, such as making the decision to fire those 300 people.

Consider the predicament. There are families that will be impacted. The surrounding community will take an economic hit. People who get laid off instantly pull back on spending at stores, restaurants, car washes, and salons. And you will be target No. 1 for making the decision to let those 300 people go.

If you think in those terms, you're human. But don't take it too personally. Today, things change more rapidly. If the division had been able to perform and draw a good profit every year, it would still be intact. On the other hand, if the division loses money, it can't go on forever. Sometimes you have to cut your losses and move on.

How do you fire 300 workers? It isn't easy. Once the decision is made, and only after the oversight team has exhausted its search for any and all solutions, make the necessary preparations. Put together a statement explaining why the decision was made. Share it with the affected workers and their families, as well as the world at large. Resign yourself to the fact that no one will be happy.

Be prepared for personal attacks, either verbally or physically. In some cases, you may need added security for yourself and the company's management team, as well as for physical assets such as branch offices, factories, stores, or warehouses.

Be sure to offer a path forward for the affected workers. Sure, you can issue a statement and then the 300 people are gone, but don't leave them twisting in the wind. Go the extra mile and set up an outside relationship with a recruiting firm. Encourage the workers to visit the recruiter, update their resumes, and attend city- or state-sponsored retraining programs, as needed.

If managers are let go, most often they will be offered a severance package — typically reduced pay and benefits for six months or until such time as they find a new job. Hourly workers also may receive a severance package, but not always.

If you receive a severance package, it may be illegal to collect unemployment. If you are caught double-dipping, the government can issue heavy fines or proceed with criminal charges. In some countries, severance packages are very strictly

regulated. In the United States, most employee handbooks detail what constitutes a severance package. In almost all instances, an employee who agrees to a severance package must sign a statement asserting that they will not sue the company for wrongful dismissal. If they do, the severance money must be returned.

If you get fired for an irresponsible act like releasing confidential information to a competitor, don't count on a severance package. In fact, you may be charged with embezzlement and thrown in jail.

The act of firing 300 people and the resulting aftermath will be stressful, so make sure to prep important constituents beforehand. Granted, you don't want the news leaking out before you tell the affected workers; if that happens, chaos will ensue. But before you make the announcement, inform key managers, area politicians, and other affected parties an hour or two beforehand. Ask for their confidentiality before sharing the information.

No one likes bad news, but if you spring it on everyone all it once, be prepared for pushback. To make things a little easier, let key people know ahead of time that the decision is coming, and provide the reasons why the decision was made.

The people on the other side won't like the news, but at least you respected the relationship and gave them a heads-up. No one likes to learn of bad news after the fact, whether in a newspaper or as part of a TV report. If that happens, it shows the company is inept, callous, uncaring, and/or ruthless. Most people, including talented people who make a company function, will leave. Recruits will avoid the company, as well.

By maintaining cordial relationships with business, nonprofit, government, and union leaders, bad news can be handled as compassionately as possible. It's a terrible hardship to fire someone, let alone 300 people. But sometimes you have to take one step back to move two steps forward. No sugarcoating can erase the difficulty. The best thing to do is minimize the damage and help those workers find their next calling.

At times, there's no guarantee that the decision to close a factory or a division will move forward. Depending on the circumstance, the bad news could encounter stiff union or government resistance. After all, many unions use their clout, and the dues they collect from workers, to support politicians loyal to their cause. That's a tough one-two punch.

Consider the consequences of unions and politicians working together. When the French automaker PSA Peugeot Citroen announced in July 2012 the layoff of 8,000 workers and the closing of a factory due to a deep drop in demand, newly-elected French President Francois Hollande stated he would not let the company carry out its plans (France and other European countries compounded the problem by offering consumers incentives to buy new cars for a period of time, which pulled sales forward).

Backed by unions, Hollande accused Peugeot of letting its workers go so the management team could pocket the savings. In reality, the company had to do something or risk defaulting on its debt and possibly being swallowed up in bankruptcy court.

Here we have a classic case of unions spending mightily to get certain politicians elected, and then using their influence to direct government policy. Companies like Peugeot are often caught in the middle.

As director of labor relations at a company in the crosshairs of powerful unions and myopic politicians, be prepared for a bitter fight. You will need every contact possible to get through it. Be sure to bring in the experts and consult with those companies that have successfully navigated such turbulent waters. It may well be the difference between success and defeat.

In the best of all worlds, create a solution that benefits everyone. Instead of taking on an adversarial relationship with the government and union leaders on the other side of the table, think about a solution where everyone wins. The other side will often resort to gutter politics and try to smear your company — and you — in the mud; don't go for it.

Take the high ground. Keep offering solutions such as working with the government and unions to identify new employment markets and industries for the employees, or suggest retraining programs. Make sure those workers learn new, marketable skills. Work with educators to pinpoint expansion markets, and encourage business incubation and accelerator programs to promote entrepreneurialism. Encourage the government and universities to work together with you to identify opportunities. If the other side doesn't like your ideas, ask for theirs. Eventually they will lose the battle for public opinion, if all they do is attack without offering solutions.

As it stands, the French automaker is proceeding forward with the layoffs and the plant closing. The union promised to fight the decision, likely with a massive strike at other Peugeot facilities, while Hollande and his administration sought to pass laws that institute stiff monetary penalties for any French company that fires its workers. The latter initiative, if allowed to pass, will only encourage French companies to relocate their operations elsewhere, while any new company looking to invest resources in France will be extremely cautious.

The outcome of such a law is more unemployment. What company in its right mind would hire workers knowing that they will have to pay a stiff penalty if they eventually let those same employees go? Not many, I suspect.

What's more, consumer sentiment in France is waning. Public opinion polls taken after the Peugeot episode showed a marked decline in consumer confidence as people questioned the ability of government to effect positive change. If a government gets too large, it becomes unwielding and inefficient. A strong, free market-driven economy has proven time and time again to be the best creator of wealth and efficiency.

The takeaways? Build and mine your database. Stay humble. Don't get in the gutter with your opponents. Be a visionary and find solutions that limit as much damage as possible. Add value.

4 GOOGLE THIS!

IF YOU SERVE AS A CFO OF A MAJOR CORPORATION, BE CAREFUL. YOUR BOSSES MAY WANT TO PRESSURE YOU INTO OVERLOOKING AN UNEXPLAINED EXPENSE, FORGIVE A LOAN, OR WRITE A CHECK TO THEIR FAVORITE CHARITABLE ORGANIZATION.

Social channels are great as long as what you post can be reviewed in any boardroom in America.

That's not to say you can't have fun on your own time. But when you're representing the company, be on your best behavior. You want to come off as polished and professional. Funny works when people laugh or take notice in a positive way.

If you intend to be the life of the party, be careful. If you drink too much, things can backfire quickly. For one thing, it's likely you won't remember much the next morning. That is, if there is a next morning.

Consider what might happen at a holiday media party hosted by a major corporation: A reporter drinks too much, attempts to drive home, and gets lost. In this instance, the reporter should have asked a friend for a ride home, or hired a cab or sedan service.

As it turns out, the reporter flips his car on the freeway, is injured, and spends several weeks in the hospital recuperating. Needless to say, the reporter could have killed or injured someone. What's more, the reporter opened the corporation hosting the party to a potential lawsuit for over-serving alcohol.

The story never makes the papers, and a lawsuit is never filed, but an ambitious TV reporter wouldn't hesitate to play up such an incident. Imagine if the story led the newscast the next night?

If you find yourself the subject of negative media attention because of a drunk driving charge or some other mistake, the only way out is to apologize profusely to all parties affected, including the general public. And make sure it never happens again. As the saying goes, those who don't learn from history are doomed to repeat it. Volunteer to attend alcohol-counseling classes and be prepared to donate time and money to a worthy cause such as a drug treatment and rehabilitation center.

When you are attending a party hosted by a company or organization, drink sparingly — or not at all. Make sure to eat something. In addition, be aware of the alcohol content of a given drink. The alcohol percentage of beer ranges from 3-10 percent; wine, including fortified wine, is 8-20 percent; liquor and spirits range from 15-98 percent.

If you drink too much, catch a ride with someone or call a cab. Better to be safe than sorry. You don't want to draw attention to yourself because of a bonehead move.

On the other hand, if you are trying to attract attention, tread slowly.

If you have a new product or service, a well-crafted YouTube video can work wonders. But remember to review it among close friends or trusted associates before launching it to the world. You don't want things to backfire. Be open to change. It's rare that something is perfect the first time out.

Don't believe it? Get the original outtakes of any song. A band or performer will go through multiple takes before releasing a song.

Consider that the Beatles didn't become popular until manager Brian Epstein saw them perform live in Liverpool in 1962. Prior to that, the band played in relative obscurity. They made two rather uneventful tours of Germany.

What they lacked in popularity, the lads made up for in persistence. In those early days, they had a van with no windshield. During the winter, each of the boys would take his turn driving while the others piled up in the back to stay warm.

What drove them was a simple phrase from band member John Lennon. When things looked bleak, John would yell out: "Where are we going, fellas?" And they would answer, "To the top, Johnny!" And John would respond, "Where's that, fellas?" And the group would yell out, "To the toppermost of the poppermost!"

The Beatles went on to become arguably the most popular rock band of all time.

But it all started with the pursuit of a dream.

It's the same in your corporate or personal life. Strive to be the best.

Be on your best behavior. Don't go AWOL (a military term, Absent Without Leave). Consider the Detroit judge who sent pictures he took with his cell phone of his bare-naked chest. He sent them to a female colleague. He came close to being thrown off the bench. While he was quick to apologize, he has since been suspended without pay over a conflict of interest in a case pending in his court.

Remember, you're always representing the company.

If a client is looking for a great time, deliver a great time. It doesn't have to be multiple cocktails over lunch or dinner.

Don't let your ego get in the way. You don't have to be the life of the party, especially if it doesn't come naturally. Drinking more won't make you smarter. In fact, it just makes you dumber.

At the same time, don't get caught in the corporate bubble for too long. Sure, it's great to work for a successful company, attend power lunches, and mingle at exclusive art exhibitions or inside the 50-yard-line suite at a professional football game, but never lose sight of the fact there are many less fortunate people living around the world.

Learn to give back. Stay humble. Don't get caught up in proving to the world that you're the smartest person on the planet.

Consider what happened to Dennis Kozlowski, the former CEO of Tyco International. During the late 1990s, Tyco was riding high due to a major expansion effort and a roaring stock market. Kozlowski, it seems, could do no wrong. But the good times didn't last.

Kozlowski drew too much attention to himself after it was learned he received more than $80 million in supposedly unauthorized bonuses and almost $15 million in art, and he had allegedly directed $20 million in Tyco funds to a former director, listed as an investment banking fee. The payments, whether legal or not, caught the attention of state prosecutors in New York. In the first of two trials, the case ended in a mistrial after a juror claimed she felt threatened by someone from the general public.

In the subsequent trial, in 2005, Kozlowski and Tyco's CFO, Mark Swartz, were convicted and sentenced to eight to 30 years in prison. The pair was convicted of falsifying business records, grand larceny, and securities fraud, among other crimes. At the second trial, Kozlowski could not explain why he neglected to report on his 1999 tax return a $25 million loan from Tyco that was forgiven.

In 2007, Kozlowski's appeal was unsuccessful. Today, he resides in a New York correctional facility. He filed for parole in spring 2012, but the application was denied. His next chance of parole is in late 2013. If he fails that hearing, he could well be in jail for the maximum term of his original sentence, meaning he won't get released until 2030. Born in 1946, Kozlowski will be 84 years old upon his release.

Legal pundits can argue the merits of the case, but the reality is Kozlowski went from a high-flying CEO to an inmate. To make matters worse, he resides in a state prison (federal prisons are typically nicer and less restrictive). As news of Kozlowski's lifestyle began to leak out, the media had a field day.

Consider that for his wife's 40th birthday party, Kozlowski invited guests to Sardinia, an island off of Italy. Since Kozlowski and others directed that the party double as a shareholder meeting, Tyco paid half of the $2 million cost. Reports show the extravaganza included an ice sculpture of Michelangelo's "David" urinating vodka, as well as a concert by Jimmy Buffet.

During the trial, a video of the party was shown. Whether the video played on the minds of the jury is an open debate, but it likely didn't help matters.

If you serve as a CFO of a major corporation, be careful. Your bosses may want to pressure you into overlooking an unexplained expense, forgive a loan, or write a check to their favorite charitable organization. What's more, the executives above you may try to mix business with pleasure by bringing their friends on the corporation's Gulfstream 5 and claiming it as a business trip, which the company would pay for. Since you're in charge of the corporation's finances, you must scrutinize every last bit of spending. What's more, publicly traded transactions must be reported to the U.S. Securities and Exchange Commission.

If there's one area of a corporation that requires constant vigilance, it's the finance department. Some prosecutors salivate over the prospect of nailing an executive team with fraud or grand larceny. Such nefarious acts are wrong, and most prosecutors love nothing more than to win "a trial of the century" to ensure their re-election or boost their aspirations for higher office. That's why so many prosecutors go on to become mayors, legislators, or governors. America loves a crime-stopper.

On the other hand, prosecutors can go too far, in my opinion. A. Alfred Taubman built up the nation's finest collections of luxury shopping malls starting in 1950, and led an investment team that in 1983 acquired and privatized Sotheby's, the prestigious art auction house in New York. In 1988, the company went public again, trading shares on the New York Stock Exchange.

The challenge for Taubman, who ran dozens of businesses, was oversight. More and more, he relied on managers to run his various operations, including the 77,000-acre Irvine Ranch, located in southern California. Taubman and a group of investors acquired the property for $350 million in 1977 and sold it six years later for $1 billion. He also co-owned the Michigan Panthers football team and A&W Restaurants (acquired for $4 million in 1982 and sold for $20 million a dozen years later).

In most cases, running the businesses in this way worked out well. But putting too much power into the hands of others, if not monitored properly, can be risky. For a period, Taubman owned the department store chain Woodward & Lothrop, but he had to sell it because some of his key managers lost interest in running the business.

Taubman admits that one of the big reasons he was convicted on a single count of price-fixing in 2001 for allegedly directing Sotheby's CEO Diana "Dede" Brooks to collude on the setting of commissions with rival Christie's auction house was that he wasn't minding the business on a daily basis.

As it turned out, federal prosecutors offered Brooks a deal to implicate Taubman in the price-fixing scheme she had cooked up with Christie's CEO Christopher Davidge. Numerous media accounts after the trial pointed out the unfairness of the proceedings, and the fact that at least one member of the jury felt "coerced" by other jury members to enter a guilty plea against Taubman.

Taubman took it all in stride. After spending nine months in federal prison, the corporate titan wrote his memoir, *Threshold Resistance*, and focused on various philanthropic activities. He has donated millions of dollars to numerous causes, including educational endeavors at the University of Michigan, Wayne State University, Harvard University, Lawrence Technological University, and the College for Creative Studies. In addition, he's been a generous supporter of the Detroit Institute of Arts and other museums.

He's also provided millions of dollars for medical research, primarily at the University of Michigan, in hopes that people like Dr. Eva Feldman and Dr. Yehoash Raphael will discover treatments for Lou Gehrig's disease and deafness (Taubman has suffered from hearing loss for years).

If there is anything that has defined Taubman throughout his 60-year business career, it is the excitement and pleasure of acquiring and enhancing a company or endeavor.

"Are entrepreneurs born or created through circumstances?" Taubman reflects for a minute. "I think it's a combination of both. Don't be afraid to fail. Take the plunge, but only when you're ready and you have fully researched the correct course of action. And make sure everyone is taken care of. It doesn't pay to leave people in the lurch — and, quite frankly, it's bad manners."

Leaving people in the lurch is bad for any business. There are plenty of people who don't care about public opinion or personal consequences. They'll post embarrassing photos of business leaders, sports stars, politicians, or celebrities. They'll spread rumors or initiate a lawsuit to put people in a negative light or collect a settlement.

As a general rule, don't post embarrassing photos or videos on the Internet. Use a camera wisely. Need proof? Prince Harry of England was caught naked at a wild party in Las Vegas in August 2012. I'm sure he had a great time, but after the incident landed in the London tabloids, there's been nothing but shame and regret.

And as the civilian drone industry develops, be aware that there will be more cameras in the sky.

As a strict rule, don't post pictures of your client in an unflattering light, such as throwing down a shot of whiskey or being involved in some other potentially embarrassing act. What will his or her boss think — let alone your client's network of colleagues, relatives, and friends?

If you post a photo or video that doesn't go over well, take it down immediately and apologize. Remember, there's only so much damage control you can do. If you upset a client by posting an embarrassing moment in his or her life, kiss your next contract or purchase order goodbye. Better to post a photo of your client with a celebrity or a VIP, or with a group of people having a good time.

Scott Monty, global digital/multimedia communications manager at Ford, sums it up nicely: "What happens in Vegas, stays on Google."

Be careful what you post. Chrysler dropped one of their ad agencies after an employee tweeted @ChryslerAutos: "I find it ironic that Detroit is known as the #motorcity and yet no one here knows how to f-----g drive." In turn, the employee was fired by the ad agency.

Keep the bigger picture in mind when you're encouraged to do something. When someone asks to take your picture, inquire where the picture will appear. It may be that you don't want your photo taken, especially if the photographer represents a newspaper that has been critical of your company or your career.

Let's face it: Newspaper and TV reporters can be very aggressive. And, at times, they make huge mistakes. Or they twist the facts and splash a hyped-up report on the front page or in the opening segment of a newscast. What the photographer may really want is a goofy picture of you. Be careful.

If you are at a charity event and the picture will be used for the organization's website, or perhaps in a local lifestyle or business magazine, it's often a safe bet that things will be fine. But keep in mind the picture can be copied by another media outlet and used in a negative light.

In this case, the goofier the photo, the better for the news organization. How many times have you seen a terrible picture of someone who is being attacked or held out by a newspaper or TV news outlet? They do it on purpose.

So outside of a photography studio, how do you ensure all of your public photos look professional?

It takes a little prep time to ensure a great image.

If you have a glass in your hand, set it down or hold it down by your waist or behind someone's back. Do the same with a cigarette. Cigars are OK, and even better if you're at a cigar party. But take the cigar out of your mouth. Most people look better with a cigar in their hand.

Just before the camera flashes, lean your chin forward a bit and give a big smile. Show those teeth! A big smile is contagious. People want to be around people with big smiles.

If you have bad teeth, get them fixed. If not, there's no reason for a straight face. Smile. Let people know you're having a good time.

If you're at a social function and a professional photographer asks to take a group shot, be sure to remove your nametag. Gentleman should button their jackets. It makes for a much more professional photo. No one wants to see someone's gut hanging out. And be sure to adjust your tie.

Ladies should give their best pose, but don't overdo it. If you're pursing your lips and drawing in your cheeks, you'll look like a fish. Practice with a trusted friend or in front of a mirror so you present the perfect look every time.

PHOTO TIME:

1.
REMOVE
NAMETAG

2. BUTTON
JACKET,
STRAIGHTEN
TIE/DRESS

3. SET FOOD
/DRINKS TO
THE SIDE

4. SMILE,
SHOW THOSE
TEETH

5.
EXTEND CHIN
SLIGHTLY
FORWARD

If your spouse or close friend is next to you, it's OK to face that person, say at a 30-degree angle. Don't turn in too much though, as the picture will only show the side of your face.

Be sure to stand up straight. Level your eyes to the camera. If you look up, people might think you're conceited or self-absorbed. Pretend a good friend is about to walk through the camera lens. Give your best greeting.

Despite the potential for a bad news story, it's good to have a few party pictures of yourself on the Web or in a respected magazine, especially for people looking to meet you for the first time, and vice versa. If they see you at a charitable event, believe me, they will be impressed.

If there's a photo out there that you don't like, call or e-mail the source and ask them to remove it. In most cases, they will. If they don't, keep trying. They will eventually get sick of you and take the photo down.

For a video interview, practice turning from the camera to the person asking the questions. Don't look up or down, or from side to side, too often. You want people to know that you are engaged and sincere, no matter the issue.

Consider hiring a speech coach. If you're giving a speech and are unsure of how to craft a poignant message, hire a ghostwriter.

On a related front, always be on guard.

If you are picking your nose and a camera catches it, you could be the subject of ridicule for weeks (if you need to take care of something in private, head to the nearest restroom).

Whether you're in school or out in the professional world, take a class or two to learn how to speak effectively in front of an audience and on camera. There is a difference. For most people, it's harder than it looks.

Remember to practice giving slow and measured responses. You don't want to come off as scatter-brained or excitable. Be sure to enunciate your words. If you speak too fast, your interview will wind up on the cutting room floor. For more detailed information about conducting an effective interview with a reporter, please visit Chapter 11: Media Training.

5 COMMUNI-CATIONS

DON'T GLOSS OVER THE PROBLEM, DON'T IGNORE THE PROBLEM, AND DON'T BLAME YOUR PROBLEM ON SOMEONE ELSE.

Learn to write. Whenever someone provides you with a memorable evening, a fine meal, or sterling service, send a thank-you note. An e-mail or Facebook post is great, but a hand-written note on personalized stationery always hits the mark.

Because people so seldom write anymore, a short note can go a long way.

Or, reversing gears, an employer like Google might provide a written test as part of the hiring process. It may even be timed.

For stationery, make sure to select heavy stock paper with your name or initials. Your company may provide it for you or, if you're the owner, make sure everyone has access to nice letterhead with the company logo, street address, telephone number, and website.

For a more formal follow-up, type the response and have it printed on your stationery. If you're looking to establish a personal relationship that could lead to a business deal or new connections, send a hand-written note.

If you or your company makes a mistake — and let's face it, we all screw up at some point — a well-crafted response can alleviate a lot of damage. Be clear and concise, never presumptive or opinionated.

Explain what happened, how you plan to fix the problem, and follow through to make sure everything is done correctly. Don't gloss over the problem, don't ignore the problem, and don't blame your problem on someone else.

Don't blow people off when they have an issue with you, or your company. Like an untreated wound, a problem that festers only gets worse.

Don't give people the opportunity to badmouth you all over town, send angry letters to the media, or post a grievance on one or multiple social media channels. If you are in the wrong, fess up right away and apologize. In most cases, the problem will go away in a few days.

Remember the two-week rule.

Most people forget what happens after two weeks. Think about what you had for dinner two weeks ago, whom you had dinner with, and where. It's hard to recall. But don't assume things will get better just because two weeks went by. If you've failed to rectify a problem, it only gets worse.

So how do you correct a problem?

Be proactive; people will appreciate it. In most cases, you should send a handwritten apology, along with a plan of action stating how the problem will be fixed.

You may want to include a small gift like cupcakes, flowers, or a gift certificate to a nice restaurant. Most people will accept the apology and move on.

Take the same approach if you've caused a problem inside your office. Be willing to work extra hours at no pay to reduce the impact of any damage you caused. Learn from the experience. What could you have done differently?

If you take all the right steps and the other person or party is still bitter, it's time to move in a different direction. Sometimes a problem won't go away, so mitigate the fallout.

Consider the awful scene of the BP oil spill in the Gulf of Mexico. Eleven workers were killed when one of the company's drilling rigs exploded in April 2010. Another 17 workers were injured. The damage to surrounding aquatic and marine life, along with the tourism and fishing industries, was immeasurable. Under strong encouragement from the federal government, BP set up a $20 billion trust fund to compensate victims; according to various news reports, more than $10 billion has been paid to claimants to date.

The company's CEO at the time, Tony Hayward, initially downplayed the potential damage. After numerous complaints, he issued an apology some six weeks after the accident.

Why it took six weeks to issue a formal apology is anyone's guess, but it was far too long.

The spill released an estimated 200 million gallons of oil. After several other misstatements, Hayward resigned as CEO in October 2010. While the formal apology came off as sincere, too much time had elapsed. It should have been done right after the spill, in my opinion. And sometimes, no matter how sincere the apology, the public will demand that someone is fired or forced to resign for their role in an accident. That's just reality.

In another instance, a routine apology can come off as insincere.

Without much forewarning, Netflix announced plans in July 2011 to hike fees for customers of its "DVD by mail" service. The move upset thousands of people, and didn't play well in the media. A few weeks later, in September, Netflix CEO Reed Hastings sent customers an e-mail which, at first, came off as a sincerely written apology.

But within the body of the e-mail, Hastings said the new price structure charges would stick and, by the way, the DVD rental service would be transferred to a separate entity called Qwikster (never mind the company didn't have a Twitter account set up yet).

Next, Hastings explained Netflix would remain an ongoing concern by offering streaming video only. The apology wasn't really an apology; rather, it was an announcement of Netflix's new payment policy and the fact that there now would be two companies that customers had to navigate separately. That meant two accounts instead of one, two bills instead of one, two passwords instead of one, and so on.

Following heavy customer backlash that saw the cancellation of thousands of accounts, Netflix reversed course and left things relatively the same save for a higher rate — from around $10 a month to $16 a month.

Surprisingly, Hastings survived the media onslaught and customer backlash. One of his saving graces was the fact that he co-founded the company. Had he been a CEO appointed by a board of directors, it's likely he would have been let go for overseeing the loss of thousands of accounts and the resulting sharp drop in the company's stock price.

The lesson here is to address any negative activity or comments that come your way as quickly as possible. Make sure multiple people are involved in any apology that is made. Had Hastings better vetted his apology, which was actually an explanation of a price hike disguised as an apology, it's likely the company would have never offered to split into two distinct parts.

In this instance, Hastings' apology benefited the company and not the consumer. He put himself first.

For any apology you offer, make sure it's for the right reasons. You are attempting to right a wrong. The goal is to make the consumer whole, or as nearly whole as possible. You definitely want to add value to the consumer.

Whenever you propose to change a service or product, be sure to conduct plenty of consumer focus groups. Have people from outside your industry sign nondisclosure agreements and ask their opinion of your proposed plans.

Your company, or a third party, can conduct the interviews — although if the inquiry is done in-house, there is the potential that the conclusion will already have been arrived at. After all, most employees have a natural loyalty to the boss, and they may fear any bad news will not be taken well. It can be the same with a third-party company that conducts focus groups.

The best advice here is to find a proven and impartial group to handle the focus groups, whether internally or externally. My preference is to have a third party conduct them, as they are more likely to be impartial. If the third party tends to skew bad news, they likely won't last long. I recommend conducting a consumer focus group for most product introductions or changes in service.

At times, a move in a new direction will be controversial from the outset. Stay on message. Sometimes it takes a while for people to accept change. Be ready to explain your side, whether you're appearing before the media, attending a cocktail party, working out at the club, or playing a round of golf.

Recall the controversy that swirled around Augusta National Golf Club. The prestigious course, located in Augusta, Georgia, hosts the Masters Tournament each year. Since the club was founded in 1933, and up until August 2012, no women members were allowed. The club had every right to preclude women members, much as other private organizations like the Girl Scouts, Boy Scouts, fraternities, and sororities.

In 2002, Martha Burk, the chair at the time of the National Council of Women's Organizations in Washington, D.C. (and now director of its corporate accountability project), wrote a letter to Augusta National stating that its male-only member-

DID YOU KNOW...

JAPANESE BUSINESS CUSTOMS:

1. BOW AS LOW AS YOUR HOST

2. ACCEPT A BUSINESS CARD WITH TWO HANDS

3. EXAMINE CARD, DO NOT PUT IN A POCKET

4. AVOID THE NUMBER 4; IT MEANS BAD LUCK

5. WRAP ALL GIFTS; AVOID WHITE PAPER (SYMBOLIZES DEATH)

ship policy during a very public event like The Masters constituted sexism. The club denied the accusation, and refused to be bullied into changing its membership policy. Burk said she would insist that sponsors boycott the tournament.

In response, the club's then chairman, Hootie Johnson, sent a three-sentence letter to Burk explaining that the club would not budge from its membership policy. He then issued a three-page letter to the media outlining the club's position.

Burk, fanning the media attention that surrounded her letter, decided to set up a protest during the tournament the following year. As it turned out, the attack fizzled and there were likely more members of the media at the protest than there were protesters.

The lesson here: Don't let the other side control the message.

Augusta National was clearly in its rights to confine membership to men. Johnson made the right move in releasing the letter to the media. He got the club's position out for everyone to see. In many ways, the letter took the wind out of the sails of the protest.

In August 2012, Augusta National admitted its first female members — former Secretary of State Condoleezza Rice and South Carolina financier Darla Moore. Burk, in subsequent media interviews, took credit for the change, saying she "knew we could outlast them."

When you're battling for control of a certain topic in the media, be sure to get your side of the story out there. Post your side of the issue on your website, Facebook page, etc. Write letters to the media explaining your position. Get out and conduct TV and radio interviews.

But be careful. Members of the media may try to bait you into saying something stupid. Or they may try to twist your words around. Take things slow. Members of the media are very good at firing several tough questions in a row. To better prepare yourself, hire a media expert and practice responding to rapid-fire questions. As you will find, it's best to consider each question individually and provide thoughtful, measured responses.

You can prepare notes, if need be. If reporters keep harping on a certain issue, direct them to your previous written statement(s) on the issue. Or call them out by saying: "I know you've asked that same question several times; please refer to our comments about the matter. That's all I'm prepared to say."

It also pays to understand the other side's position, and point out to the media and other interested parties any flaws in a dispute. In the case of Augusta National, Burk was trying to make a name for herself. If she really cared about promoting exclusion-free clubs, she would have addressed the Girl Scouts, Boy Scouts, etc.

Switching gears, consider how you might accept an apology.

How would you react if someone spilled a drink all over you, insulted your spouse, or failed to deliver a product or service?

Be gracious. Recognize that people make mistakes and allow them the time to fix the problem.

But don't be too forgiving.

Allow people to apologize, and if it's sincere, accept it and move on.

No one likes to hear people bring up the same problem again and again. If someone keeps mentioning a problem that you truly bent over backward to rectify, mention what you did.

If someone with a past grievance sees you at a cocktail party, be cordial. If they bring up the past, mention how you fixed the problem. Apologize, once again, and make sure people know it — "Dave, I'm sorry, I want to apologize again. That should never have happened. I know we fixed the problem to your satisfaction. Did you enjoy the champagne we sent?"

Always try to convert a negative into a positive. In life, there are winners and losers, and the losers become winners when the winners show the losers how to be the winners.

CHAPTER SIX

THE END RUN – OFFICE POLITICS

WHETHER YOU'RE A CEO, A SALES REPRESENTATIVE, OR A JANITOR, EVERYONE IS PART OF THE COMPANY TEAM. LEARN TO UNDERSTAND AND APPRECIATE EVERYONE'S TALENTS, AND WHAT THEY BRING TO THE TABLE.

Be wary of anyone who says, "Well, that's the way we've always done it."

If the people you work with, whether professionally or as part of a group or a nonprofit organization, are resistant to change, be careful. Don't be afraid to find solutions and get your message through to the decision-makers.

On the other hand, be delicate.

You have to work with people on a daily basis, and it can be incredibly stressful if you're seen as the one always stirring the pot. What's more, it can be tough on your career aspirations. Pick your battles wisely. You could be passed up for the next available promotion because you showed up your boss one too many times.

Let's face it; office politics can turn nasty.

Envy and jealously are powerful emotions, and some people can't control their actions.

Remember, you were hired to perform a job. Do your job.

Don't give anyone an opening to take your job.

In the same vein, watch your back.

Someone may be conspiring to take your job or blame you for his or her problem. Recognize first that such people have low self-esteem; otherwise, they would have gathered the necessary humility to admit their mistake and set about finding a way to fix it.

I recall one colleague, an associate business editor, who inserted an error in one of my articles. She added information to the story that indicated a land development company had purchased a piece of property to build a large shopping mall.

The real story was that the property owner — in this case, a municipality — selected the developer as the "preferred developer."

They had yet to agree to the terms of a land deal, which actually was never consummated. When I pointed out to the editor the following morning that the land had yet to be purchased, she wanted me to submit the correction.

I refused, even though she was my immediate boss.

If I had submitted the correction, it would have been entered into my employment file. That, of course, would impact my annual employment review and could conceivably drag down any potential increase to my salary.

I stood my ground. She wound up submitting the correction. The reason was the computer system we used tracked all the changes to a given story. She couldn't refute it, but I suspect if she had found a way to make me submit the correction for the next day's paper, she would have done it.

I didn't make a scene. I simply held my ground. In this instance, the person who made the error reported the error. Don't let people run over you.

Remember, though, it can't always be done in the office.

You can't keep running to your boss or the executive wing every time there's a problem. Try everything in your power to fix it yourself.

If that doesn't work, an "end run" can come in handy.

There's nothing wrong with attending an outside event that draws key executives at your company. Learn what these types of events are, either by asking around or searching the Internet for chamber of commerce meetings, trade shows, company retreats, or charitable events.

Get to know what makes your company tick, and be sincere in your support.

If you're just getting started in the corporate world and your company is hosting a social event, volunteer to pass out nametags or serve as a greeter. It's a good way to show your commitment to the company, plus you'll get to know key people your firm reaches out to such as clients, vendors, regulators, or politicians.

Attending an event outside the office with top-level executives to rectify a problem or to suggest an improvement your boss is reluctant to make can be tricky.

You don't want to be seen as working outside the system — which, in reality, is exactly what you're doing.

Here's how an end run works: Once you see a key executive at an outside event, strike up a casual conversation and quickly work your way to the problem or challenge at hand.

Suggest the change you're seeking in a positive way; perhaps it will save money or boost efficiency. Watch very closely for the executive's reaction. Do his or her eyes light up a bit, or do they grow heavy and dreary? Wait for the executive to agree or disagree.

If done properly, the executive more than likely will take ownership of the problem or opportunity and drive it forward with your assistance.

If, on the other hand, the executive disagrees, inquire as to why. Stand your ground, be professional, and never raise your voice.

Perhaps there was something you overlooked. If that's the case, learn from it and move to a different topic. There will be other end runs in life, but again, pick your opportunities wisely.

Whether your end run works out or not, don't dwell too long on the outcome.

Don't cover the same ground or, as they say, beat a dead horse.

Move on.

Show the executive how valuable you are. Yes, you didn't meet your goal of changing a service or outcome, but at least you tried. Plus, you learned from it.

This can all happen in the span of five minutes, so you need to have a well-thought-out plan. If your end run doesn't work, what's next on your list? When the conversation is over, bow out graciously and wish the executive a nice night or weekend.

Obviously, you can't attend the cocktail party, seek out the executive, have a conversation, and then immediately leave because you are upset that your idea got shot down.

Make yourself useful by continuing to network and learn. Don't be afraid to seek out new business or ask for assistance. That's what networking is for.

If your company provides consulting services, such as government relations, be sure to let people know. Stay on message.

INTERNAL OFFICE GUIDE:

1. OFFICE CULTURE IS EVERYTHING; MAKE IT POSITIVE

2. COMPANY/ GROUP/DIVISION ACTIVITIES **ONCE A QUARTER**

3. END-OF-THE-YEAR **HOLIDAY PARTY A MUST**

4. INVEST IN **CONTINUING EDUCATION**

5. STUDY AND INCORPORATE **BEST PRACTICES**

There's also the buddy system. Find someone at the company you can trust, and be sure to help him or her out. Set up a communication plan ahead of time, like exchanging texts (ringer off, vibrate on). Be discreet.

If one of you notices an opening with a potential client, send a message, meet up, and make your introduction.

It's easy.

Say your name, where you work within the company, and how much you appreciate the potential client's time, talents, or offerings. Don't be a suck-up, don't dominate the conversation, and don't linger.

If you've done your homework, pick a topic that interests your acquaintance and let them have the floor. This first meeting should be very brief, given the time constraints.

If things go well, by all means arrange for a follow-up meeting. As time passes, work hard to get the deal signed. If it comes through, make sure to reward your buddy.

In addition, be wary of what makes people tick. You don't want to start off on the wrong foot.

At Chrysler, Chairman and CEO Sergio Marchionne once barked at a new employee for speaking in Italian. Why?

When Daimler AG owned Chrysler, the German executives would speak in their native tongue. It was a "put down" for any American executive in the vicinity, and served to generate tension and mistrust. Certainly it was a recipe for disaster, as the Germans all but destroyed and eventually unloaded the car company to Cerberus, a private equity firm. Cerberus tried to run the company from New York — a big mistake.

When Fiat took over starting in 2009, Marchionne knew great design and engineering would only come from collaboration, not cross-country or cross-border edicts.

Marchionne knew the best way to get everyone on the same page was to speak one language — in this case, English. It's just one reason why Chrysler has fared so well since its 2009 bankruptcy. They listened, regrouped, and worked as a team.

Always remember that most CEOs are like business coaches. They meet with their department heads and work with them to improve the operations. But when you have two large companies that are going through a merger, the CEO must be a dictator. If everyone is scared of you, things will get done. Marchionne was a dictator at first, but as auto sales took off, he became more of a business coach.

Whether you're a CEO, a sales representative, or a janitor, everyone is part of the company team. Learn to understand and appreciate everyone's talents, and what they bring to the table. Stay humble. Let your work shine through. Help others whenever possible. They will notice.

CHAPTER SEVEN

THUNDER & LIGHTNING

REMEMBER, *IT IS NEVER EASY TO COMPETE WITH THE CONVENTIONS OF THE STATUS QUO — BUT THEN AGAIN, RUNNING THE RISK OF OBSCURITY IS NO CONSOLATION.*

Use thunder and lightning to your advantage.

So what is lightning? The Apple iPod, iPhone, and iPad come to mind. It's the spark of energy that creates the next innovation, or the next revolution.

Thunder is a call to action, but it must be positive.

There's no problem using thunder and lightning to advance your career or a product. Steve Jobs, the co-founder of Apple with Steve Wozniak and Ronald Wayne, was a master at creating thunder and lightning.

Create a great product and promote it to the masses. Lightning is a discharge of atmospheric electricity that can reach speeds of 140,000 mph and generate temperatures of 54,000 degrees. When lightning happens, nothing stands in its way. When followed by thunder, it's impossible not to notice.

Google, the Internet search giant, offers an amazing product. But it can't sit back and call it a day. It has competitors like Yahoo and Bing to contend with. Google must continue to deliver great products or risk ambiguity.

Remember, it is never easy to compete with the conventions of the status quo — but then again, running the risk of obscurity is no consolation.

So what does Google do to keep its name relevant? It continues to offer advertisers new products and services. It entered the mobile phone market. It's experimenting with eyeglasses that have a small computer screen in the corner of one of the lenses. There are projects like the Google Car and the Google Airplane.

The company keeps moving forward, keeps innovating, and keeps grabbing attention — thunder and lightning.

Anyone can talk loud and create a lot of thunder, especially people who believe the squeaky wheel always gets the grease.

You need to add value.

Is there anyone out there who wants his or her tombstone to read: "Best Paper-Pusher Ever"?

If you're going into politics, don't be a self-serving politician who uses the power of the office to stay in office.

Don't reward your friends and strike out against your enemies.

If you hold a government job or were elected to a political office, or even if you are a volunteer, you should do the best job possible with the least amount of resources. Period.

If you sit on the board of directors of a foundation, a charity, or a nonprofit, do not take a salary or submit an invoice for your services. You are a volunteer, not a paid employee. In recent years, the IRS has been asking board members of nonprofit associations to fill out an annual form listing any benefits they've received, business or otherwise, from the nonprofit. The IRS wants to know whether board members are benefiting from their charitable endeavors.

If you are a volunteer and someone asks you to perform a service in exchange for money, don't take the money. Give it back. You are there to help the charity.

If you do decide to pursue public office, it had better be for the right reasons.

Don't be a politician like Two-Lunch Larry. Whenever a businessperson would invite Larry to lunch, he would order two lunches — one to eat, and one to take home for later.

Larry eventually went to jail for tax evasion. He never really worked much, according to media reports. A camera crew caught up with him after a tip. It seems Larry was leaving work soon after arriving, often to go back home to sleep or run errands for hours on end. He didn't offer a lot of value, to say the least.

DID YOU KNOW...

STRESS MANAGEMENT:

EAT HEALTHY FOOD;
EXERCISE REGULARLY

JOIN ATHLETIC/ COUNTRY CLUB

STAY HUMBLE; ADOPT A CHARITY

TAKE A WALK DURING THE DAY

AVOID FOOD/ DRINKS LATE AT NIGHT

Bad karma always catches up with you.

Sometimes thunder and lightning work for a period of time, but then people lose interest.

Take, for example, the Occupy movement that was all the rage in the fall of 2011. It was mostly young students who gathered in public spaces to complain about the rich cats on Wall Street, the so-called 1 percent of the top wage-earners in America.

Many of the protestors lacked jobs or were there to support the unemployed. Others had racked up heavy debts, either from school loans or carefree lifestyles.

But the assemblies never had a long life span.

For one thing, winter was setting in, making outdoor protests impractical in colder climates. And as anyone who has lived in a temporary campground knows, health concerns crop up from the outset. Germs are spread, proper nutrition and hygiene go out the window, and disease is not far off.

You don't hear much about the Occupy movement these days. Why?

The initial thunder and lightning wore off. There was nothing new beyond the initial shock and awe. The message got stale, and the protestors failed to adapt.

They occupied public places, and the permits only lasted so long. Plus, the media became bored.

At the same time, government has a duty to protect public safety, and a temporary campground can easily develop into a cesspool.

So what should the protestors do if they want to stay relevant?

Keep the brand, but protest without advance warning. Keep everyone on his or her toes. Where will they show up next? Leave people guessing. If they do that, they'll get their thunder and lightning.

When the time is right, such as at a product launch, a new restaurant opening, or a merger with another company, be ready with the right amount of thunder and lightning. Many companies that sell retail goods will tease the media with little bits of tantalizing information.

The company might release a close-up photo of a streamlined tail lamp for a new luxury sedan. Or they make sure to leave a prototype in a popular bar, in the hope that it will reach the media. The more thunder and lightning you can create, the better the buzz on the street.

Thunder and lightning also works in a turnaround situation.

When Nancy M. Schlichting took over as CEO of Henry Ford Health System in 2003, the health care organization in Detroit was in poor financial health.

Overall, the six-hospital system, spread across the city and suburbs, was losing more than $7 million a month.

Not content to wait for a blue ribbon panel to craft and assemble a turnaround plan, Schlichting sought ideas from patients, employees, administrators, board members, and volunteers. In short order, the hospital undertook inexpensive cosmetic improvements — painting parties, flower plantings, and fundraisers. New uniforms were ordered.

Simultaneously, Schlichting asked her management team to identify the best practices in health care, research, technology, services, medical offerings, and hospitality. Schlichting also was determined to open a new hospital in West Bloomfield, a Detroit suburb. But she didn't want an ordinary hospital; she wanted an organization that would be a global leader in wellness, productivity, operational efficiency, culture, and financial performance.

Before Schlichting hired an architect, she took the time to work with physicians, nurses, medical professionals, and support teams to learn how to improve care, lower costs, boost efficiency, and limit ambulatory visits by helping to fund clinics within neighborhoods. She also sought to improve educational outreach to maintain and improve public health.

At the same time, she began to formulate a vision of a health care laboratory in West Bloomfield. The challenge was finding a visionary like herself to carry it through. Looking across the hospital's management team, Schlichting centered on one of her volunteer board members — Gerard van Grinsven, at the time general manager of the Ritz Carleton in the nearby suburb of Dearborn (he holds a bachelor of science degree from The Hotel Management School in Maastricht, The Netherlands).

So what inspired Schlichting to hire someone with no medical or health care experience to design, build, and run Henry Ford West Bloomfield Hospital? "Gerard wasn't on my radar screen when we first started planning West Bloomfield, but ... I observed he was a tremendous leader," she says. "He came to me one day and asked about some career advice, and he said he was attracted to health care, and even then I didn't think of him. But it eventually occurred to me that he had the skill set to transform traditional hospital thinking and really embrace wellness. I just didn't know he would excel at it."

Hired in 2006, van Grinsven initially used his time to pore over nutritional research, especially as it concerned food grown organically or via hydroponics. He also studied holistic healing practices like acupuncture and water therapy, as well as theories regarding indoor noise and natural light levels, and the latest in telecommunications equipment — research that convinced him to broadcast specific medical information to Internet-enabled televisions in each of the hospital's 192 private suites.

He also embarked on an arduous travel schedule. Close to home, he tapped into the private archives of automotive pioneer Henry Ford, the founder of Ford Motor Co. and Henry Ford Hospital, for information on wellness. Having grown up on a farm in Dearborn, Ford developed a life-long passion for nutrition. Van Grinsven also visited organic farms in Michigan and the Midwest, sat down with nutritional experts, interviewed thought leaders and health care experts, and consulted financial experts to ascertain how the new facility could generate profits that would assist Henry Ford's entire hospital network. The latter goal comes amid a medical environment known for strict cost controls such as set reimbursements for most procedures.

As he planned the hospital and oversaw construction, van Grinsven left nothing to chance. Hearing from a colleague that the team planning food service at the hospital was holding a meeting to discuss operational needs, van Grinsven slipped into the gathering unannounced. He listened intently as a kitchen staff member explained that there would be dozens of deep-fat fryers and a large amount of cubic freezer space. At that moment, van Grinsven started thinking about greasy French fries and chicken fingers — frozen food that would be thawed, cooked, and served to patients. Stepping forward to introduce himself, van Grinsven refused to blame anyone directly for following the standard operating procedures of nearly every hospital in the world.

Rather, it was at that moment that he set out to turn the entire hospital system on its ear. Instead of building a facility to respond to illness, disease, or complicated maladies like obesity or smoking, the West Bloomfield hospital would promote wellness at every turn. That meant, as his culinary staff soon learned, that there would no deep-fat fryers or freezers, save for a modest unit that would be used for sorbet. "Ladies and gentlemen," van Grinsven announced in his rich Dutch accent, "we are going to transform the hospital system for the betterment of the human race, and it starts right here."

Today, the hospital locally sources and prepares organic food, and offers patient rooms and amenities that rival a five-star hotel, including a spa, wellness retail offerings, and a greenhouse where lettuce, tomatoes, peppers, and other vegetables are grown and served to patients, staff, and visitors. Meanwhile, each of the 192 private suites is equipped with state-of-the-art equipment, including a flat-screen TV that offers a patient specific information directly related to their respective operation/treatment.

He also established the Vita Wellness Center, which provides patients with a health coach. There's a stadium kitchen where patients, family members, and the community can access healthy cooking demonstrations and wellness programs. The hospital, designed after a northern Michigan resort, also offers a series of indoor storefronts that mimic a quaint village.

To transcend the fixed-cost environment as well as provide cutting-edge services, van Grinsven embraced a novel way of hiring employees. For the 1,100 jobs the West Bloomfield hospital would initially create when it opened in March 2009, he had applicants — including those from Henry Ford Health System — undergo testing and interviews to ensure that they would excel in a nurturing, team environment defined by better information-sharing, excellent communication practices, and electronic medical records. "Seventy percent of medical errors happen due to poor or limited communication," van Grinsven says. "We are now well below that average."

In addition to adopting many of principles of Henry Ford West Bloomfield Hospital — following Schlichting's original vision — Henry Ford Health System formed the Innovation Institute in collaboration with Wayne State University, the College for Creative Studies, Carnegie Mellon University, the University of Chicago, and the Universidad Complutense de Madrid. The Institute, which opened in October 2011, brings together medical researchers, designers, and engineers to create for-profit companies that will soon begin producing a wide range of medical devices, including robots.

Designed to be a conversation-changer about Detroit on a global level, the facility is housed in a three-story, 38,000-square-foot building that opened in 1924 as an educational center for student nurses. Henry Ford will generate revenue by licensing new patents and taking equity stakes in some of the for-profit businesses formed and incubated. In addition, doctors and hospital executives will act as angel investors. The intent is to build new production facilities from the spinoff research and development on Henry Ford's Hospital's growing campus in Detroit.

Eyeing the future, Henry Ford West Bloomfield Hospital has started to educate visiting business and government leaders, pre-med students, and other health care constituencies while, at the same time, consulting with medical organizations around the world that seek to replicate its successes.

Other consulting topics include how to execute a successful turnaround while encouraging behavioral changes that lead to continuous operational and employee efficiency gains, cost reductions, and better decision-making. In addition, in partnership with the Detroit Medical Center and Wayne State University, Henry Ford Health System recently unveiled an employee incentive program to entice workers to move near and around its Detroit campus. The program has been incredibly popular.

At the same time, Henry Ford employees have organized a support network among local and national initiatives, including American Red Cross blood drives, the American Heart Association Heart Walk, the Juvenile Diabetes Research Walk, and disaster relief efforts. Employees also are encouraged to donate to any of 170 different Henry Ford programs and initiatives. In 2011, nearly 56 percent of physicians and employees pledged a record $3 million toward the various community partnerships.

So what's next?

As reports surface of increased life expectancy, Henry Ford is striving to develop breakthroughs that will slow the aging process by way of a healthy diet, exercise, drugs, and genetic therapy. Researchers also are working on new ways to replace worn-out organs — and even to help the body rebuild itself. To boost patient services, the hospital offers multiple diciplines (a sort of one-stop shop) that include such offerings as the Josephine Ford Cancer Center, a Bone and Joint Center, a Heart and Vascular Institute, the Vattikuti Urology Institute, and a Center for Women and Children's Health, among others.

A future blueprint of added wellness services and offerings will be provided as Schlichting and her team bring about an expansion in West Bloomfield that will offer more patient suites, a boutique hotel and conference center that caters to business and nonprofit leaders around the world, and new retail offerings.

Here's how it would work: During a management retreat or strategy session, each guest will receive an in-depth physical. Along with the examination, guests will walk away with a personal nutrition plan, a workout regimen, and any number of spiritual disciplines they may want to pursue, such as yoga or meditation.

In the grand scheme of things, Schlichting had a vision that represented thunder and lightning in an industry often resistant to change. Things only began to undergo a transformation when van Grinsven, an outsider, brought to life one of the most innovative hospitals in the world. Seven years after Schlichting began leading Henry Ford Health System, the organization went from producing losses to recording $60.1 million in net income in 2010, on revenue of $4.1 billion.

For its efforts, Henry Ford Health System was one of four 2011 recipients of the Malcolm Baldrige National Quality Award. Named after the 26th secretary of commerce, the award was established in 1987 by Congress to promote quality awareness while recognizing exceptional business achievements.

And it all began when Schlichting had the confidence to throw convention out the window and open the door to a good idea.

CHAPTER EIGHT

THE ONLY REASON ANY COMPANY ENTERS BANKRUPTCY IS THAT IT HAS RUN OUT OF CASH.

Be willing to meet with almost anyone to advance your career or take things to the next level.

In the spring of 2009, I received a call from a former Kmart executive asking if we could meet up for coffee. Kmart was one of the top two retailers in America since its meteoric start in 1962 through the early 1970s. Along with Sears, Kmart personified and perfected the art of selling to the masses.

But in the mid-1970s, Kmart lost its way. Store managers were treated like mini-emperors so that top management had little control or oversight (management actually encouraged store-level autonomy).

No one could tell the store managers how various products were to be displayed or how inventory was to be tracked. Can you imagine all the different "books" that were kept? The integration of computers at Kmart was delayed for years for fear of upsetting the store managers.

Eventually, in 2002, the once-mighty retailer entered Chapter 11 bankruptcy, having run out of cash due to mismanagement, "yes" people on the board of directors, and perhaps the most inefficient and ugly corporate headquarters ever constructed. Made up of 23, three-story office pads connected together in a giant triangle, it would take someone 10 minutes to walk from one end of the building to the other. Just think how much productivity was lost each day by people literally walking around in circles.

For Kmart, it was one misadventure after another. There were misguided acquisitions like Builder's Square, Sports Authority, and Borders Books, among others. Kmart expanded outside of their core operations. It's like a family with one child that, within a two-year period, adopts seven teenagers. Unless the parents are incredibly organized and disciplined, chaos will ensue.

Eventually, Kmart emerged from Chapter 11, and a new management team began to right the ship. In 2005 it was sold to Sears, and the operations moved from suburban Detroit to suburban Chicago.

So why would I agree to meet with a former Kmart executive in 2009?

I had plenty of other things to cover and, as a general rule, the media likes to look ahead. Still, in the end, history is the greatest power when measuring a company's value. Fortunately, my curiosity got the best of me. As I prepared to meet the gentleman for coffee, I began to recall Kmart's problems.

People like Chairman and CEO Joe Antonini fell in love with the corporate lifestyle. And as is often the case, as the leader goes, so goes the rest of the company — especially within the management ranks.

At Kmart, a lot of it was about appearances, not deeds.

Antonini was fond of wearing very expensive, hand-tailored Italian suits with gold accessories. It's always a good idea to wear accessories like cuff links, bracelets, watches, and necklaces in good taste.

I've seen plenty of corporate people and politicians who wear well-tailored suits and lots of jewelry, but they have very little idea of how to operate a business, a division, or a political office. They dress the part, but offer little else.

If you meet someone like this, your red flag should slowly start to rise. If the flag gets to the top, avoid the person as best you can. Say hello, compliment them on their attire, and move on. In almost all cases, the person will fail.

But always be nice, as you never know when that person can help you down the road. It may be a reference, a referral, or a good tip about what your competition is up to.

Another point to consider: An executive can afford to wear expensive clothes and accessories, but when a politician is dressed immaculately, it immediately raises concerns. If they came from wealth, well, there's no problem. But if they don't have the relative means to afford fine things, they're likely raiding their campaign coffers to buy Armani suits, gold jewelry, and Cartier eyewear.

Or they're accepting lots of gifts in exchange for favors. Such practices could be considered a bribe, which will draw the attention of prosecutors.

Back at Kmart, the sheer irony — which Antonini obviously didn't appreciate — was that he never seemed to like to wear what was offered in the retailer's men's department.

It was as if the stores were beneath him, both from an operational level and a social status level.

Imagine if he had used his appreciation for Italian suits — literally rolled up his sleeves — to work and sweat alongside his merchandise team to develop the finest suits at various price points.

Now spread that energy across multiple divisions.

He really could have created a lasting image that Kmart was working hard to offer quality products at affordable prices to deserving consumers.

Instead, Antonini rarely left the safe world inside the corporate bubble. Nor did his immediate staff. They didn't venture out, solicit advice, or take chances. It was so bad that Antonini asked Lee Iacocca, the former chairman and CEO of Chrysler who led the automaker out of bankruptcy in the early 1980s, what he was doing wrong.

Iacocca's response was that Antonini ought to look in the mirror.

Yes, Antonini would visit an occasional store. But the visits were orchestrated press affairs in which the store manager had weeks to prepare. It's interesting how a Wall Street analyst or a retail writer from a major newspaper can see all the problems brewing at a company like Kmart yet, despite all the warnings in analyst reports or articles on the business pages, the management team continues its destructive ways.

The only reason any company enters bankruptcy is that it has run out of cash.

One of the biggest problems Kmart encountered was fighting management hubris. They believed they could do no wrong. If there was a problem, they said the strategy they selected was never carried through properly. It was always someone else's fault when things went wrong.

Winners identify the problem and make the tough decisions to right that which is wrong.

When you're up against a Kmart situation, where a division or the entire company

DID YOU KNOW...

FINE DINING TIPS:

1. MAKE RESERVATIONS DURING SLOW HOURS

2. HOUSE/ CHEF'S TABLE IS BEST

3. CALL AHEAD TO DECANT WINE

4. HAVE WAITER HANDLE VALET

5. TIP BASED ON LEVEL OF SERVICE

is suddenly losing money due to falling sales or rising material costs, it's time to bring in the experts.

In fact, you should be consulting with experts all along.

Form a board of advisors when you're just starting out in high school or college. It's a group of trusted people in various fields of business or scholastic studies. You could even add a politician. Understanding how government thinks and acts can be very valuable. In most instances, government is slow to act and is rarely as productive as the private sector.

Meet with your advisors as a group, although it's often easier to meet one-on-one over a meal or coffee — once every three or four months should do it. If problems are brewing, however, you will want to meet more often. As you enter the corporate world, add new advisors as you see fit.

Don't ever think that you know everything.

Fight hubris at every turn and embrace humility. Don't be afraid to ask questions, even if it may appear to the other person or group that you are weak. You are learning, and they should recognize that. It's all about the product, not the person.

When I met the former Kmart executive for coffee, there was some initial chatter about the state of the once-mighty retailer. As we worked past the initial subtleties of trust, he explained that the smarter executives knew that Kmart was heading for bankruptcy.

In 1999, three years prior to the bankruptcy, some of the executives took buyouts. They had had enough. Kmart, as most companies do in such situations, offered the exiting executives legacy benefits such as health care insurance or stock options. The only caveat was that each executive had to sign a 10-year nondisclosure agreement.

What does that mean?

For a period of 10 years after accepting a buyout package, an executive is barred from speaking in public about what happened during their time at the company. That means they can't write books, talk to the media, or post online. If the nondisclosure agreement is violated, the company can ask for the amount of the buyout package back.

During the meeting, it quickly became apparent that the Kmart 10-year nondisclosure agreements from 1999 were winding down, or had just expired.

The executive explained that Kmart's former chief technology officer was living and working in Denver and was willing to talk about his time and experience at Kmart.

As we reached out to the chief technology officer and other executives, I read Bob Ortega's book, *In Sam We Trust*, about Wal-Mart founder Sam Walton. It's a book I highly encourage anyone to read. From the small town of Bentonville, Arkansas, Sam Walton built Wal-Mart into the nation's largest retailer. In the early 1980s Kmart gave Walton — who they believed, at the time, was a regional retailer confined to the Southeast — free reign of its headquarters for a day. Walton was able to delve into Kmart's shipping, distribution, and delivery operations.

With that backdrop, we developed a feature, told for the first time, about the contributing factors that led to Kmart's bankruptcy.

It was one of my favorite features to edit (Norm Sinclair was the writer), and we were able to bring a great deal to the table due to Sinclair's insightful writing and Ortega's book. Because I accepted a meeting invitation I wasn't sure would lead anywhere, we produced an excellent review of what not to do in business.

The feature went on to win the 2011 Gold Medal for Best Explanatory Journalism from the Alliance of Area Business Publications. Again, the business lesson can't be stated enough.

Be willing to meet with just about anyone to advance your company or your career.

What's the worst outcome if things don't work out?

Hopefully, you'll pick up something of value, a little nugget of gold: How to act, what to avoid, or, at the very least, a nice cup of coffee to temporarily take your mind off the pile of work waiting for you on your desk.

9 NET-WORKING

BLACK TIE *MEANS A TUXEDO OR AN ELEGANT DRESS. DO NOT UNDER-DRESS FOR A FORMAL EVENT. IT MAKES YOU LOOK INCREDIBLY CHEAP, SELF-SERVING, AND UNCARING.*

Networking is one of the toughest arenas to master — so many events, so little time, and lots of agendas.

Before attending a meeting, a business conference, a press event, a wine tasting, or a fundraiser, research it on the Internet. Who attended last year, who will be honored this year, what's the dress code, how long will it last, and what's the best time to arrive? And leave? These are all key enablers for success.

If it's an event at a private residence, there may be some information about the dwelling online, but assume the setting will be upscale unless it infers otherwise. A Super Bowl party, book signing, or barbecue means business casual, which calls for nice slacks or jeans, a shirt or blouse, and perhaps a jacket if it's cold out. Nice shorts work, if it's hot.

Google Maps or another Web tool can provide an image of the residence and a lay of the neighborhood, or drive by a few days before the event if the residence isn't located in a gated community.

To work a room successfully, you need to dress the part.

Black tie means a tuxedo or an elegant dress. Do not under-dress for a formal event. It makes you look incredibly cheap, self-serving, and uncaring. Your hosts have requested black tie, and you must respect them.

For gentlemen, a tuxedo or two is a great investment. For starters, it's always in the closet, ready to go. There's no fumbling at the tuxedo rental store or worrying whether your rental shoes or pants will actually fit.

Think of all the time wasted renting a tuxedo, along with the money. At a fine store, a well-appointed tuxedo costs less than $1,000. If you attend 10 black tie events in a year, the payback is quick. For ladies, four or five elegant gowns are an absolute must.

If the event is black tie optional, dress up but don't feel you must wear a tuxedo or a gown. But if you're on the board of the organization, or a close friend of the host, wearing formal attire is a sign of respect. Certainly, if you're seated at the head table or on a dais, black tie is a must.

Black tie optional doesn't mean dress down. A dark suit with a nice shirt and tie is perfectly acceptable. But jeans don't cut it, even if you have a nice shirt and a jacket.

Dress too far down at your own risk.

For nicer clubs, learn the rules. Major athletic and social clubs require a jacket or tie for most events, or in special areas like a main dining room.

Follow the rules.

A fine club, in order to attract and retain a sophisticated membership base, sets standards. Most frown on denim, but may allow it temporarily before or after a professional football game, or a similar event held nearby. After all, the club can't chase away too many people or they'll miss out on food and beverage sales.

A quick note: Keep all of your club memberships under your own name, even if your employer pays for them. That way, if you ever leave your job or are let go, at least you still belong to the club. That's very important when it comes time to find a new job.

If it's a casual event, go casual. If you're unsure, bring a sports jacket and tie. You can leave them in the car, or check them at the coat desk. You certainly don't want the club providing a jacket or tie, as they often don't fit or don't match.

Remember, sophistication and success go hand in hand.

For business casual, something nice is recommended. A jacket, sans tie, is a nice touch. For events like a house party held in tandem with a sporting event on TV, support the local team. That means themed polo golf shirts, pullovers, hats, etc.

Don't wear sportswear that will offend the host or their guests. If you're a fan of the St. Louis Cardinals baseball team and you're in Chicago on business, leave your Cardinals gear at home. If you attend a Chicago Cubs game in your Cardinals gear, you're asking for trouble.

People can get very worked up about sports, and if your goal in attending an event is to land a big contract or establish a merger, it can go sideways if you're inside the owner's suite cheering and supporting the other team.

Keep your passion for a particular team to yourself, unless it's the home team. It's the same for major brands.

Don't wear a Coca-Cola shirt to a party hosted by a Pepsi Cola distributor.

Don't wear a GM hat to a party thrown by a Ford executive.

Even if you don't like a certain product, you may find that suppressing your distaste, however difficult it may be, will lead to good results. You may not like a certain computer, but you can land a major software contract because you said nice things about it.

Better to be pleasant than to ruin any chance of making a deal.

Just remember, in two weeks you will most likely forget about the substandard computer because you're too busy fulfilling a multimillion-dollar software contract in tandem with a major update by the computer maker.

Plus, you'll be receiving congratulations from all of your associates, including your boss and your boss's boss.

Keep in mind that if you screw up at an event, at a meeting, or at a grocery store, there's always the two-week rule. Nobody remembers much after two weeks have gone by. If you had a food stain on your shirt, most people won't remember it after two weeks because there's too much information to process.

Unless something really bad happens, things will usually blow over. People will remember a drunk, a bumbling fool, the fumbled speech, or one of the worst things of all — body odor.

Business is done by deeds, not predictions.

Always look your best. Proper grooming is a must, and proper manners are essential.

The higher you climb in the corporate world, more is expected.

For example, never bite your nails in public. It's a sign of weakness. People instinctively know you have a stress issue, such as nervousness, and people generally don't like to hang out with anyone who is nervous.

I've been to major luncheons with a large dais and watched in horror as people, typically men, chomp on their nails during the keynote speech. It's rather embarrassing, to say the least, especially when it's your boss or CEO.

Don't pick your teeth with your nails. I've watched plenty of people, including senior executives, use their pinky to remove a piece of food from their teeth during a meal, and then turn around a minute later and greet someone with a handshake.

Such behavior shows a complete lack of respect. It also spreads germs.

When you have a piece of food stuck in your teeth, excuse yourself and go to the bathroom. Or carry a toothpick in a small case. Never pick your teeth with your hands in public and then continue greeting people.

If worse comes to worst, use a napkin to casually remove a piece of food lodged between your teeth. Pretend you're wiping your mouth. It may not always work, but it's better than nothing, especially if you can't leave the table because the main speaker is giving his or her address.

Ladies have it easier in this example, as most carry a small mirror in their purse.

If you notice a poppy seed lodged between your two front teeth, it's best to excuse yourself and head to the nearest lavatory.

Perhaps you've tasted something not to your liking, or you're served olives that aren't pitted. What to do? Use your fork and transfer that piece of fat, the olive pit, or anything else you don't like to a side dish.

Don't spit it in your napkin.

If a waiter comes by and picks up your napkin while you're away in the bathroom, disaster could ensue. That piece of food or olive pit could go flying across the table and hit your boss's husband right in the face. I've seen it happen. People will get very upset if chewed food hits them.

So you've arrived at the big party. What to do first?

Check in and get your nametag and seating assignment. If you're wearing a suit and a receptionist hands you a nametag sticker, place it on the widest part of your suit lapel. Do not place the sticker so that it's attached to both your lapel and your suit. As you shake hands to greet people, the sticker will quickly fall off due to the movement between your lapel and your jacket. Keep it on the lapel.

Another option is to put it on the front of your suit pocket, typically over your heart. That never fails, unless it's humid and windy. In those instances, stick the nametag on your shirt or blouse. When you head inside for dinner, place the nametag back on your suit lapel or pocket.

As you check in, scan the room for familiar faces or people you recognize and would like to meet. If you know a lot of faces, but a name or two doesn't register (we all forget), think of your keyword for that person and look it up on your smart phone under the contact list you created.

Most times you can figure out the person's name by searching under a certain company. I use this trick all the time. As you're searching for someone's name in the middle of an event, all anyone knows is that you're looking at your smart phone.

Most everyone likes to be greeted by first name, so this trick pays off tenfold.

Once you're inside the event and you've met several key people during the cocktail reception, what happens if you arrive at your table for dinner and all the seats are taken?

Obviously, someone is at the wrong table — or someone crashed the party. If the nametags have table numbers on them, you can figure things out pretty quickly.

People who don't have nametags may very well be crashing the party. If you can't discern who shouldn't be at your table, ask a volunteer to assist.

Three things will happen. Either they will figure out who doesn't belong and have them reseated, or the volunteer will guide you to another table where there's an open seat. If this is a hardship, don't make too big of a scene.

You still will be served dinner, and you're free to mingle between courses. Plus, your new table partners might prove interesting or lead to a deal down the road.

You never know.

The other option is to have the wait staff add another chair at the table you're supposed to be seated at.

Sure, things will be tight, but don't make a big deal about it.

Comment about something positive like the weather, a recent announcement that benefits your city, a sports victory, or the event itself.

People will settle in soon enough if things are interesting and lively.

Ask simple questions. Comment about the event, the organization, or the facility. What other topics can you choose to get a conversation started? Does the person seated on the right or left of you prefer red or white wine? Perhaps it's a certain cocktail? Where is their family from? Where do they live? Do they have any hobbies? Do they plan to go anywhere warm for the winter?

So many people go to events and don't network; they stay with people they know and never venture forward other than by chance.

That's not good, unless you're renewing old acquaintances.

Don't be afraid to walk up to people you don't know and introduce yourself.

In most cases, avoid cutting off intense conversations. Be sure to provide your business card if asked, or volunteer your card. You never know where it might lead.

If you're talking with a group of people, be mindful of others who are standing by themselves. It's easy to introduce someone new to a group, especially if you know everyone. Once you make the introduction, share each person's title and organization. The person new to the group will be grateful and, who knows, it may lead to a mutually beneficial relationship.

So often I see people wandering around a party with no one to talk to. Be a big brother or a big sister, and get to know them. They might be new to the area, the company, or the particular event. Any number of positive things can result. Be productive. Build your knowledge base.

What happens if you're seated next to someone who doesn't speak your language, or doesn't have great command of your language? Look around to see if someone nearby is fluent in both languages, and pull them over. Do the best you can to find common ground. Use your smart phone to communicate if there's a total language gap. There are plenty of apps that offer quick assistance, like Google Translate.

If someone has limited command of a language, ask where they're from. Pull out your smart phone and show them where you live, and ask them to show you where they live. Once you've established their homeland, look up the top exports, agricultural products, or sports teams.

Remember, you're always building your knowledge base. Don't sit in silence, and don't allow anyone else near you to sit in silence.

At most events, people are seated at a round table offering 10 seats. When you arrive at your table, introduce yourself to everyone. Act as the unofficial host of the table.

As more guests arrive, make the introductions. It can be difficult to remember everyone's name, especially if there are no nametags, but do the best you can.

One trick is to create a keyword for each guest. Perhaps Mary is wearing a maroon jacket, so Mary Maroon. Or Pete has a bow tie, so Bow Tie Pete. You also can jot the names down on a piece of paper, or arrange everyone's business card in front of you in juxtaposition to where they're seated.

As soon as you sit down at a restaurant or an event, place your napkin in your lap. It signals to everyone that you are sophisticated and fully prepared to enjoy a fine meal. Don't allow a waiter to set a napkin in your lap. It makes you look weak and helpless.

GREEN ROOM ETIQUETTE:

1. GREET EVERYONE IN THE ROOM

2. AVOID DISCUSSING POLITICS

3.EAT SPARINGLY; USE MOUTHWASH

4. WATCH THE SHOW, RIDE THE ENERGY

5. RELAX, YOU MADE IT THIS FAR

A good way to set a napkin on your lap is to form the linen into a triangle, with the base of the triangle along your waist. Or you can place the entire napkin over your lap. I prefer the triangle. If the dinner is especially messy — say you've been served barbecued ribs — you can use one side of the napkin and, when it's soiled, you can flip it around and form it into another triangle.

By doing this, the soiled side never rests directly on your pants, skirt, or dress. Don't be afraid to request extra napkins from your server.

Before we get to the utensils, remember that your bread plate, along with a butter knife, will be on your left. It's the same arrangement if the place setting includes a charger — a decorative, often monogrammed, plate that other plates will be served on.

Glasses for water, white wine, and red wine will be on the right (and possibly a sherry glass or champagne flute).

A coffee cup and saucer, if provided before dessert, will be on the right, as well.

One way to remember the general layout is that your starches (bread plate) will be on the left, while all of your glassware will be on your right.

So often I see people sit down and reach for the nearest water, not knowing they've taken their neighbor's glass. Rookie mistake, for sure. Remember, your water glass will always be on the right. As a point of good manners, my friend Patricia LaFrance adds that ladies should wipe off any lipstick left on a glass or coffee mug. "It's your responsibility to keep your glass clean," says LaFrance, operations manager at Spa Renaissance in Troy. "Otherwise, it makes you look bad."

When the first course arrives, don't start eating until everyone at your table has been served.

Follow the same rule for every subsequent course.

Typically, ladies are served first.

Most often, the first course is a salad. If there are rolls on the table, reach out and take one and pass the basket to your left. Remember, you're the unofficial host. It's the same with the salad dressing bowl (there are often two types of dressing on a table).

If the dressing doesn't make it around, be sure to ask someone to pass it along. It's the same with the rolls, the butter dish, and the salt and pepper.

Worried about which fork or knife to use with your salad or appetizer? Check out the table setting diagram on Page 121.

Always use the utensils set on the outside first, and work your way inward.

If the first course is a salad and there are two forks set to the left of your plate, use the fork on the far left first. It's often the smallest fork.

Sometimes there are three or more forks. Again, use the far left fork first, and work your way in. If the first course is shrimp cocktail or escargot (cooked land snails), the smallest fork will be on the far left if the table was set correctly (sometimes it is on the far right).

Be aware that not all table settings follow these rules. It all depends on the person leading the wait staff. The vast majority of place settings, however, follow the diagram.

As the next course arrives, use the next set of silverware. At most dinners, there are two forks on the left and two knives on the right. The outer fork and outer knife are for the salad, while the inner utensils are for the main course.

If there are two forks and one knife, use the knife for both the salad and the main course. To keep from soiling the tablecloth, and potentially your sleeves, wipe the knife off as best as you can on the salad plate when you're done eating.

Next, set the knife so that it rests nicely on the clean fork. Don't allow the waiter to touch the knife, as they will often set it on the tablecloth. Also notice that the serrated part of the knife should face the plate. It's safer that way.

A spoon or two may be on your right, as well. The larger spoon is for your soup (sometimes a spoon will be provided as the soup is served). The inner spoon at your place setting is reserved for coffee or tea. For dessert, a fork and spoon are often set in front of your plate. Don't use them until dessert arrives.

If you're seated and the meal is served buffet-style, wait until a waiter or volunteer comes to your table and invites everyone to the food line.

If you're planning a buffet-style party for more than 100 people, ask the wait staff to sequence the serving of the food. By sequencing the guests, you avoid a long line and it's easier for the servers to replenish trays of food, both hot and cold.

In addition, a buffet-style event costs less than a sit-down dinner. The reason is there are fewer waiters and kitchen personnel.

If you have a food allergy, let your waiter know. Don't be shy. In most cases, it's a conversation-starter. For instance, I'm allergic to garlic. So I'm not shy about asking a waiter whether any of the dishes will be prepared with garlic. People to my left or right will often overhear the conversation and make a comment. Congratulations, you got the conversation going.

CHAPTER TEN

10 EVENT PLANNING

GIVE YOURSELF PLENTY OF TIME. WELL-RUN ORGANIZATIONS TYPICALLY START PLANNING FOR NEXT YEAR'S EVENT THE WEEK AFTER THE MOST IMMEDIATE FUNDRAISER WAS HELD.

GAME PLAN

If you are planning an event, whether a company anniversary or a benefit fundraiser for a charity, demand the finest service from the banquet facility, hotel, or conference center. Costs can add up quickly, so set a budget and be mindful of prices (more on this further down). Take notes on everything, and keep a running tally of the expectations you have and whether the venue can meet all, or most, of them. Once you're satisfied, get a signed contract that lists any damages that will be covered if things go wrong.

Make sure the venue carries insurance and ask what it covers. If it's a limited policy, it might be best to select another venue. In some instances, your company or organization may need to purchase an insurance policy. This is a good time to get a lawyer or an experienced event planner involved.

Any event where alcohol is served should be insured. Let's face it; people like to have a good time. To keep people from getting drunk, consider serving beer and wine only. Some people are bound to over-drink. Make sure everyone has a sober driver to take them home. Have a cab or courier service on standby. In some cities, there are companies that will offer two drivers. One driver will take a guest home, followed by the other driver with the guest's car. It's a great service.

The alternative is not pretty. It's a crime to drive under the influence of too much alcohol. The worst thing that can happen is a drunk driver kills other people. Major property damage can also be a risk.

If someone gets drunk and is pulled over, the authorities will suspend their license, issue thousands of dollars in fees and fines, seize the vehicle, and add points to a license (which greatly increases the cost to insure a vehicle). If this happens to you, hire a good lawyer to protect your rights.

If you're planning to drink at an event, be sure to consume plenty of water, soda, or juices. The main reason anyone wakes up with a hangover is due to low hydration. As a general rule, have one glass of water or soda for every drink.

Still, everyone is different. Some people become tipsy after two drinks. If you see a friend starting to get tipsy, encourage them to drink water.

Stay organized. If you're planning an event for the first time, form a planning committee. Is it a one-time event or something that will be repeated year after year? Think about the moving parts. It's very similar to planning a wedding. Where and how will the guests arrive, how will they be greeted, where will they stand or sit, and is there a silent auction or live auction, or both?

Ideally, the planning committee should be made up of committed people who have experience in one or multiple disciplines. Someone might be in charge of transportation, another person covers food and beverage, while someone else oversees signage and sponsor needs such as a luxury car that will be displayed in the main lobby of a hotel during the event.

Seek out experienced volunteers for your planning committee. What's more, your committee will have subcommittees. A subcommittee focuses on specific tasks such as promotion, registration, or sponsorships. Provide updates to all of the committee members every two or three weeks. E-mail typically works best. It should be a progress report detailing how many days before the event, what money has been raised, and what money still needs to be raised. If the goal is to raise $200,000 for a charity, provide a running tally of what funds have been raised. That way, your committee knows if a certain task needs more work.

Businesses and nonprofits unaccustomed to producing conferences, exhibitions, or celebrations should hire an experienced event manager, says Jason Huvaere, president of Paxahau Productions in Detroit. The company produces, manages, and promotes corporate and entertainment offerings in North America and Europe, including the Movement Electronic Music Festival, Detroit Restaurant Week, and the Detroit Jazz Festival, among many others.

"No matter how confident and controlling the hosting organization, you still need an experienced manager to oversee the event and make sure everything is checked off," says Huvaere. "Don't assume anything on the budget until you have actual receipts and invoices for production, talent, management, and venue-related expenses. If costs get out of hand because you failed to properly oversee the budget, don't assume someone will rescue you at the end with sponsorships."

Once an event manager is vetted and selected — ask for referrals and conduct a background check — set a realistic event budget. There are two ways to set a budget: Rely on the event manager to perform every task, or solicit bids for all major expenses. On the latter point, event production companies have been known to double-dip, meaning they charge a management fee and then steer business to favored companies that mark up their products or services. To counteract doubling-dipping, require transparent invoices from all vendors and contractors.

"The size and scope of the event will dictate costs, and an experienced event company will work with the client whether the bidding process is mandatory or not," Huvaere says. "We've produced events for more than 15 years, so we know the right people and companies for audio and visual equipment, talent, contractors, and venues. The other major consideration is making sure the event goes off perfectly. The client should have as few concerns as possible. Their responsibility is to see to their guests."

GUEST ARRIVAL

As you're planning an event, keep the experience of each guest in mind every step of the way.

Will most people arrive by car? If so, it's best to have a valet operation in place with plenty of drivers.

If the valet company is a problem year after year, your guests will catch on. They will arrive sooner and leave earlier. That's a major issue when you have a silent or live auction. The bids will be fewer and, typically, lower.

Is the valet check-in area covered in case of inclement weather? If not, consider renting a canopy. No one likes to stand in the rain or snow, or endure high heat or severe cold, especially in formal attire. Make sure there are multiple traffic lanes at the valet area. You don't want traffic spilling out onto a main road because there's only one check-in lane. Cars sitting on a main road are an accident waiting to happen.

Consider having a company or individual sponsor the valet. In exchange, give them an advertisement in the program and have their sign(s) displayed as people drive in.

At the registration area, make sure there is plenty of room. One note about running a registration table: Have enough volunteers to check people in quickly. There are few rookie mistakes more annoying than a long check-in line.

When people pay hundreds of dollars to come to an event and there are two greeters at a table checking in 600 guests, the overall confidence level falls considerably.

Spread things out. "Overstaff" the check-in table with volunteers. Have a few roving volunteers to guide people to the correct check-in area. If there's an issue with a name, move the people aside and connect them immediately with a designated volunteer. That way the line doesn't get backed up. Put the table numbers on the nametags, as people tend to forget.

Arrange the nametags in alphabetical order. Put up large signs to designate the letter groupings: A-F, G-K, and so on. Have a couple of extra people available to monitor the tables and address any concerns.

Also, be mindful that some people like to crash parties.

It happens all the time, especially when times are tough.

If you catch someone sneaking in, kindly ask him or her to leave. Most places have security if things get out of hand.

The more room and staff there is for the check-in, the better experience it is for your guests. Don't put the registration tables in a tight space.

Guests tend to arrive in waves, so be prepared. If the line to your black-tie gala is more than 10 people long, you don't have enough check-in staff. And if the line extends outside, weather could be an issue.

In one instance, I arrived for an automotive design conference that was being held at a restaurant on the top floor of a hotel. More than 400 guests were to be in attendance. A local university served as the host. Unfortunately, there were two interns checking everyone in. They used a side hostess stand as the registration table.

As you might presume, the line quickly backed up to the two dedicated elevators. The result was that the next wave of people couldn't get off the elevators. They had to go back down one floor and take the stairs up.

Don't let this happen at your event. People will leave, never come again, or bad-mouth your organization. What should the university have done? The faculty, in this instance, was to blame.

They should have enlisted many more student volunteers. The faculty was so caught up attending to the keynote speaker that they neglected the most important duty of any host: making sure all the guests are comfortable. You wouldn't throw a party for 100 people at your home and ask your guests to wait outside as you check in each person individually at the front door, right?

CROWD FLOW

Make sure the coat check is set away from the registration tables.

Remember to think of crowd control. You want to space things out to prevent any potential bottlenecks. Be sure to have extra people at the coat check during the arrival and departure times. Another option is self-serve coat racks, but make sure there's a monitor or two. People have been known to take coats, especially if they see one nicer than their own. It rarely happens, but you never know.

In addition, if you self-park and hang your own coat, keep your car keys in a pocket or a purse. Again, it's rare, but someone can easily take a coat from a self-serve rack and walk out to the parking lot and hit a key fob until a car opens.

If you're renting a banquet facility or a conference center for the first time, set up an appointment with the staff and take a tour. Be sure to inspect the bathrooms. Are they clean, well-lit, well-appointed, and well-stocked? If so, it's a good sign the rest of the facility is clean.

Perhaps you want to hire a lavatory attendant, one each for the gentlemen and the ladies. Ask around for recommendations. Make sure the attendant is well-dressed, courteous, and has a full stock of soap, perfume, cologne, hair spray, mouth wash, candies, mints, etc.

Another concern is tipping. Do you want the bathroom attendant to accept tips, or should you pay him or her a flat fee?

I prefer a flat fee. That way, your guests won't feel bad if they don't a have a dollar or two in their pocket or purse to leave in a tip bowl. If you go with a flat fee, make sure to set up a sign or two on the bathroom counter that says "No Tipping." Below it, you can add the name of the sponsor who picked up the attendant's fee. Something like: "Tonight's attendant has been graciously provided by the ABC Corp."

SILENT AUCTION

For a silent auction benefiting a charitable organization, have plenty of volunteers to monitor the table items. Yes, people have been known to swipe a pearl necklace or a gold ring, so be prepared.

How do you set up a silent auction? If you're just starting out, it can take a few years to build up momentum. First, consider if a silent auction is right for the presenting organization. By starting out small — five to 10 quality items — you can measure the impact.

So where will the items come from? It goes back to your planning team. The auction committee will solicit items and donations from key constituents and sponsors. Most retailers are willing to donate an item in exchange for signage, a mention in the program booklet, or an advertisement.

You should recognize all of the sponsors during the event. One of the best ways to do this is to assign one or two people equipped with cordless microphones to talk up the auction items. They can mention that Best Buy donated the 40-inch flat screen TV or the XM home radio unit. The sponsors should be recognized during the formal program, as well.

Don't overdo it during the silent auction. Make sure there's light music in the background, or hire a small band or harpist. Every 15 minutes, have the volunteers talk up the auction items. You want to encourage your guests to mingle over, or near, the silent auction area. Don't drown them out with constant chatter.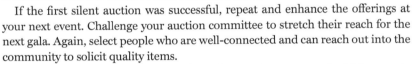

Another trick is to make sure any trays of drinks or hors d'oeuvres are served within or near the auction area.

If the first silent auction was successful, repeat and enhance the offerings at your next event. Challenge your auction committee to stretch their reach for the next gala. Again, select people who are well-connected and can reach out into the community to solicit quality items.

Overall, the committee can range from five people to 30 people. Make sure to meet periodically — conference calls are best. Solicit what each person believes they can garner in donations so that you don't have a dozen large-screen televisions (one or two is ideal). Assign someone to be the secretary and have everyone provide periodic updates.

Have a good mix of items. Consider electronic equipment, vacation packages, artwork, popular books — really, anything of sizeable value and in good taste.

The auction secretary, or someone else, must set up and maintain a spreadsheet with the following: the name of the item, a brief description, whether the item has been secured, the suggested retail price, the name of the donor(s), contact information, a tracking number, and an opening bid.

Next to the opening bid on the spreadsheet, add an adjacent column with the final bid. That way it's easy to see the financial progression and what items raised the most money. Make sure to e-mail an updated list to all of the committee members either once or twice a month (be more frequent as you get closer to the event). The list also does double duty by spurring competition. There's nothing like healthy competition within an auction committee to raise the stakes, plus everyone can see who is performing and who needs to pick up the slack.

Make it as easy as possible for someone to donate an item. Make sure to follow up quickly with any donor concerns and be prompt in sending out thank-you notes. With the thank-you note, provide a written record of the gift(s) to assist any donors who may wish to claim an IRS deduction. Consult an experienced event planner or a lawyer for more information about IRS deductions.

Give yourself plenty of time. Well-run organizations typically start planning for the next year's event the week after the most immediate fundraiser was held. It should start with a wrap-up meeting, where your planning committee addresses what went right and what went wrong.

It may be that there were too few, or too many, auction items. Or the tables were set so close together that it created bottlenecks. Make sure to spread things out, but not too far. You want people to see the items, but if they're set up in a corner where it can be difficult to view, the items won't sell.

A staff person from the banquet facility will likely have very good ideas on how to set up and run a silent auction. Be sure to walk the space with them beforehand so that you're satisfied with the placement and marketing of the auction items.

For a silent or live auction, list the items individually. Make sure everyone has a copy of the auction items, with a description, as soon as they walk in the door. This can be done within the program booklet, or as a separate listing. I prefer to place them in the program, both for live and silent auction items. For any late donations, a separate sheet can easily be slipped inside the program.

By placing the auction items in the program, people reading it will view the ads. Your sponsors will be happy.

For each item on display, prepare a bid sheet that includes most of the information from your spreadsheet — the name of the item, a brief description, the suggested retail price, the donor(s), a tracking number, and the opening bid.

Leave room for subsequent bids, and set a minimum price for each successive bid. For example, make it clear that each successive bid must be $10 or $20 more than the previous bid. That will help raise more money. Leave plenty of room for multiple bidding.

Invest in inexpensive clipboards and attach the bid sheets to them. Place the clipboards and a pen next to the corresponding item. Make sure there's room for the person's name, along with a telephone number or bid number.

If you have both a silent auction and a live auction, consider assigning a bid number for each guest. It's easy to do if you have a well-run operation that includes a spreadsheet all of your committee members have access to.

The numbers can be assigned and printed out ahead of time to speed the process. Small bidder paddles are fine, or consider having each number listed on the back of the program. Anyone who makes a bid during the live auction will wave their program in the air. To maximize the overall donations, make sure a sponsor or advertiser pays for the back cover of the program. They will love that their company name is being waved in the air multiple times during the live auction.

If you have 200 items for the silent auction, consider separating them into smaller groups and create a theme among up to 30 or so items, designated by a color or number. Or arrange the items by groups, such as restaurant gift certificates, jewelry, artwork, or sports memorabilia. It's another way to maximize the donations and make it easier for your guests to navigate the space.

Here's a good plan of attack: Open the entire silent auction at once, say at 6:00 p.m., and let everyone know that the first portion of the auction — the green area or the artwork area — will close at 7:00 p.m. Each subsequent color or category will close every 15 minutes. Make sure each area is well-located and marked, so people can easily find it.

Once an auction area is closed, have volunteers pull the sheets at the exact time. Start marketing the next themed auction area, and so on. An additional trick is to close out the least expensive items first, and work your way to the more expensive grouping of items. Another way to boost sales is to list a "Buy it Now" price at the top of each silent auction item (be sure to remove the sheet quickly once signed).

Looking over 200 items is a daunting task when you're trying to fit in networking opportunities. By separating the auction items by theme, people can work both activities into their event schedule. Plus, they have more opportunities to focus on a smaller number of items, thereby raising potential donations.

Again, make sure to pull all of the sheets once the auction time has expired. People like to hover over a certain gift as the time for bidding winds down. Be sure to give a five-minute notice, and then a one-minute notice, followed by a 10-second countdown. Part of the fun of a silent auction is allowing people to get the last bid in. For some, it's like winning a sporting event.

Silent auctions can be very competitive — which is good, overall. It means the auction committee did a great job. But if you don't pull those sheets at the designated time, some people will complain that they put in a last bid only to find

GIVING BACK:

1. VOLUNTEER FOR A NON-PROFIT BOARD/ COMMITTEE

2. DON'T USE A CHARITY TO ADVANCE YOUR CAREER

3. ATTEND/ CALL IN FOR ALL MEETINGS; SET GOALS

4. MAKE SURE NONPROFIT HAS TRUSTED ACCOUNTANT

5. PROMOTE THE CHARITY WHEN-EVER POSSIBLE

someone else was able to enter a higher bid because your volunteer staff didn't collect the sheets fast enough. You don't want to get caught in the middle of two angry bidders.

Make sure the person(s) announcing the silent auction mentions the charity or cause several times. People are more inclined to bid if they know their money is going to a worthy organization.

Prepare a script for the announcers and get it to them ahead of time. It should be straightforward, such as mentioning the charity and what each additional $500 or $1,000 raised represents in terms of helping others. For example, every $500 raised will help pay for a certified tutor for a child who has fallen behind in reading, writing, or word comprehension. What's more, let the announcer know about slow-moving items. That way, he or she can tout the bargains still available.

Another trick is to list, preferably with a photograph, all of the silent and live auction items on a charity's website. You can even hold a pre-auction on the site, say for a one-week period. When people get to the event, set the opening bids using the results from the pre-auction. In most cases, the items will draw larger bids overall.

LIVE AUCTION

The auctioneer must have plenty of experience. Generally, there are two ways an auctioneer is paid: a flat fee or a percentage of the money raised. I prefer the latter option, given the auctioneer is more motivated to draw higher bids. Sometimes, it's a combination of the two — a small flat fee and a lower percentage of the overall take.

In some cases, a donor may pay for the auctioneer. Once you've selected an auctioneer, send them the auction item information promptly — you want them well-prepared. And be sure to limit the offerings. No one likes to sit through a live auction of 50 items. Up to two dozen items is the maximum. After that, people generally get bored.

If you go with a celebrity auctioneer, such as a media personality or a sports figure, make sure the person has experience. The last thing you want is a rookie auctioneer who stumbles throughout the presentation. You also may consider two celebrity auctioneers, such as a married couple.

As a rule, you can release pent-up energy by saving the best items for the live auction. One trick is to combine multiple offerings into one package — say a week at a Caribbean resort that includes airfare, a rental car, meals, entertainment, and recreational offerings like fishing, sailing, or surfing.

Plan to have plenty of volunteers to assist the auctioneer. You don't want to lose out on a bid because the room was too large. If there are more than 500 people at an event, consider having two auctioneers.

Like the silent auction, be sure to set a minimum price and have it listed online and in the program booklet. If the minimum bid fails to draw any takers, an experienced auctioneer will immediately drop the price to generate bids. In most cases, you don't want to accumulate unsold items, so some money is better than removing the item. If a bid comes in too low, have a back-up plan. Tell the auctioneer that any low-bid items will be removed for a special online auction you're planning for one week after the event. Hopefully, it draws more interest.

If an item doesn't draw any bids, pull it. Regroup with your auction committee afterward and figure out what went wrong. The opening bid may have been too expensive. Learn from the experience, and use that knowledge the next time.

AUCTION CHECK-OUT

Have plenty of volunteers. One trick is to have a sponsor pay for the volunteer meals. During dinner, have a special table(s) for the volunteers. Another idea is to seat one volunteer at each guest table. They can act as another set of ears and eyes, plus they can promote the nonprofit organization or charity. The volunteers can raise awareness of the live auction, as well.

If you have 200 auction items (silent and live), pay attention to the checkout. People who return to the auction the following year will be more apt to bid on items if they know the check-out is well-organized. I've seen people wait upward of an hour to pay for and receive an auction item. If they have a bad experience, they likely won't return, or if they do, they'll skip the auction. No one likes to wait.

One option is to open up the check-out tables immediately after the silent auction closes. Or allow people to pay for their items as each section of a silent auction concludes. For a smaller item, your guests will have no problem stowing it beneath a chair during dinner. For larger items, be open to allowing people to pay for them ahead of time. Be sure to have some strong volunteers available to load larger items into a vehicle. Provide receipts for everything, and retain the originals for the organization's records.

Allow people to finalize the purchase of their auction items over an extended period of time. While you may run the risk of diluting the buzz of the live auction, most people attend an event with one or more people. If you have a well-organized event, your guests will figure things out very quickly. Be sure to start the live auction on time. That way, one person can run and finalize any purchases from the silent auction while their companion monitors the live auction.

You may want to separate the check-out between live and silent auction items. Create separate signs for silent auction check-out and live auction check-out.

MONEY, MONEY, MONEY

There are many ways to collect the money. Credit cards work best. The easiest thing is to take down the information and process the charges the following business day. The nicer the event, the fewer issues you will have with bogus credit cards.

If it's a more relaxed setting, where the party is open to the general public, look into renting credit card machines. There are typically a few places in every city that rent credit card machines, and they often provide discounts to charities. A landline may be needed to operate the machines.

In addition, make sure the money is deposited in the right account. I had a friend who threw a large Super Bowl party. He had other partners in the deal. They had four credit card machines to process ticket purchases, which were available for $500 apiece the night of the event. My friend, Jim, was led to believe the money raised would be deposited into a pre-agreed-upon account, but things turned out much differently.

The next morning when Jim went to access the account, he quickly learned no money had been deposited. Another partner had switched the account number with the credit card processor at the last minute. Since Jim signed for everything, he had to declare bankruptcy because there weren't any funds to pay off the caterers, the valet company, and the hosting venue. To avoid such a loss, consider setting up a limited-liability company to operate a for-profit event like a Super Bowl party. That way, if something happens to the money, the company is liable for the losses, not you.

To prevent a scam from happening, consider a credit card service that works with a smart phone. Pay Anywhere and Square are some of the options. It's easy to set up several smart phones (with people you trust). The service can alert you immediately to bogus credit cards, and it provides instant access to deposits. Have someone you trust monitor all of the transactions in real time online.

If you accept cash, be sure to have plenty of change on hand. Checks are a little more challenging, especially since banks are closed at night. If you're concerned people will write bad checks, don't accept them. Another option is to hold an item until a check clears, and then have the item available for pick-up, or drop it off.

ODDS AND ENDS

If you host an event at a hotel adjacent to a casino, there may be some restrictions. Generally, security will be tighter, meaning your guests may have to pass through a metal detector. Make sure the hotel staff has enough metal detectors and security personnel. You don't want long lines to form.

Consider setting up a VIP pre-reception party in a well-appointed room near the main event. It's another way to reward your sponsors, and you can charge more for the VIP tickets. As you plan the program, a main speaker like a corporate luminary, a sports star, a celebrity, a dignitary, or a politician can enliven the audience. If at all possible, ask the speaker if they will make an appearance at the VIP party. It will help stoke ticket sales.

Each sponsor is different. A major bank or automaker will spend their marketing dollars on certain initiatives — one year it's the Hispanic community, the next might be Asian Americans. Don't assume a sponsor will invest in a certain charity year after year. It would be nice if a major consumer products company sponsors your event on an annual basis, but that's not realistic. Since the lead sponsor is often encouraged to provide a keynote speaker, you can't have the same person addressing guests every year. That's where networking comes in handy. You need to draw new sponsors and stay in touch with existing ones. Key people come and go, so be sure to meet everyone you can at a given company or organization.

Leading up to the event, keep in mind a speaker may cancel at the last minute. Things happen, whether it's a death in the family, health problems, a major work issue, or a scandal. Always have a speaker or two on standby. If your speaker is a prominent corporate CEO or dignitary, ask his or her chief of staff for a back-up speaker ahead of time. A seasoned chief of staff is familiar with last-minute scheduling changes.

To help boost awareness of your charity event, both for ticket sales and sponsorships, consider hiring or partnering with a public relations and marketing company. The promotions company should have strong social media skills as well as traditional public relations and marketing offerings. Your organization will obviously connect all of its members, supporters, and sponsors. A good PR team can reach out to new audiences.

Another consideration is to partner with one or several media outlets. In exchange for tickets and a sponsorship, a newspaper, magazine, radio station, or TV outlet will market your event through their channels. I find it is best to partner with one media outlet per category — one newspaper, one magazine, one radio station, and one TV station. Sometimes, a publishing company will have several offerings, such as a lifestyle magazine and a business magazine. In this instance, you can partner with both. Everyone wins in such partnerships, but make sure the job gets done. If one of the news outlets drops the ball, remove them from consideration for the next event.

Be sure to gather all of your signs and other collateral material before you leave. Often, a cleaning crew will arrive later in the night and throw everything away. In addition, consider returning to the same venue each year. If a hotel or conference center did a good job, reward them by coming back. The other benefit is that you'll build up a knowledge base by returning to the same venue. Organizations that host their events at different venues each year are less efficient. It takes time to learn how to maximize your time with a given venue's staff.

CHAPTER ELEVEN

MEDIA TRAINING

IN ALL OF YOUR DEALINGS WITH THE MEDIA, THE BEST ADVICE IS TO HIRE A PUBLIC RELATIONS EXPERT TO MANAGE YOUR INTERVIEWS, PRESS RELEASES, STATEMENTS, AND OTHER PUBLIC DISCLOSURES.

Never tell a reporter your company's profits or revenue numbers (annual sales) unless you are authorized. Someone reading or listening to the story, especially someone from the IRS, may believe your company doesn't pay enough in taxes. Or a local assessor may want to re-evaluate what your company pays in property taxes, especially if you develop real estate, have large land holdings, or operate multiple commercial/industrial/warehouse facilities.

It's fine to talk about the number of employees, the success of a new product launch, or anything that puts your company or organization in a positive light.

But don't boast. People will read through it, or they'll become highly motivated to undercut your success. It happens all the time. Business can be highly competitive.

If you've signed a nondisclosure agreement, honor it. By signing the agreement, you typically agree not to tell anyone what you saw or heard. If you work in sales, and a supplier of a revolutionary medical device wants to interest you in representing their product, they will likely ask you to sign a nondisclosure agreement, also known as an NDA.

If you tell the media what is going on, they will print or broadcast the news. If people can't trust you, they won't work with you.

There are few people you can truly trust in the media. Newspapers, magazines, radio outlets, and TV stations have numerous agendas, which are as varied as the people who cover the news.

The New York Times, for example, leans Democratic. *The Wall Street Journal* tends to favor Republicans.

It's funny that a given news outlet can dish it out with the best of them, but when a rogue reporter gets called out or commits a crime, the employing news outlet will issue a brief statement or respond with a "No comment."

A reporter or news outlet must be impartial. If you ever visit a newsroom, look around. See what's posted on the walls, on the bulletin boards, and in individual offices and workstations.

If there are political campaign signs everywhere, be wary. Where's the impartiality? There should be no campaign signs or trinkets.

A reporter's job is to weigh both, or multiple, sides to a given matter and then write an impartial story. A columnist, meanwhile, is paid to provide their opinion. Both are tough jobs, with plenty of outside influences trying to spin positive coverage to their side. Those same outsiders will spin negative news about their competition or adversaries.

A reporter must be impartial. But in the news business, as in any industry, there are bad apples. For example, I know reporters who attend campaign announcements as guests. They donate money to candidates. They volunteer to hand out flyers or make calls. Reporters cannot be impartial if they're working on someone's campaign.

MEDIA RESPONSE:

1. ASK THE REPORTER WHAT THE STORY IS ABOUT

2. LEARN WHEN TO SAY, "NO COMMENT"

3. DO NOT COMMENT ON ACTIVE LAWSUITS

4. IF AMBUSHED BY A REPORTER, KEEP WALKING

5. WHEN ATTACKED, ISSUE A WRITTEN RESPONSE

If you see a reporter volunteering or working with a politician, your red flag should immediately rise. Avoid the reporter unless they really like you or your company. If you can cultivate a solid relationship that leads to good stories about your company or industry, go for it.

But be forewarned. It can always come back to bite you.

Years ago, a reporter I know actively solicited a rewards program that had just been introduced by a major corporation. I had been sent the e-mail train, so there was no doubt.

A few days later, the reporter had a change of heart and wrote a story about how the corporation tried to bribe her with free rewards points in exchange for a positive story. Nothing was further from the truth, and while the corporation denied the charge, the story still appeared in print.

The point is that reporters are human, unpredictable, and have been known to create or perpetuate a scandal to get their name on the front page.

Consider the case of Jayson Blair, a young reporter for *The New York Times* who was fired after it was learned he had fabricated articles. He claimed to have written various articles at specific places across the country when he was really at home in New York. It took months before the paper admitted to being fooled, and several staff changes followed.

Let's face it; the pressure to succeed can be overwhelming. But it never pays to deceive. Eventually, people catch on.

The good news: The Information Age makes background checks a breeze. It doesn't take long to figure out where a particular reporter stands on any number of issues. Enter the reporter's name in the keyword search of a news organization's website and his or her work will follow. A search engine will do the trick, as well.

On the other hand, it's often wise to have — or hire — a top-notch public relations staff to manage your media relationships.

You could be walking into a hornet's nest if you say the wrong thing to a reporter, or are followed and interviewed in full attack mode. I know executives who have walked out of their office, through the front door, and into the parking lot only to be waylaid. A TV reporter and a cameraperson jump out of an unmarked van for what they hope is a stinging, accusatory interview.

Be on guard. If your company is experiencing bad news, scan the parking lot for unmarked vehicles. Drive by your house before pulling into the driveway. It's the same with a condominium resort or apartment building. If you are the keynote speaker at an upcoming event, take every necessary precaution. The media has no qualms about showing up before or after an event to catch their target. Consider arriving and leaving through a back door.

Be prepared for a sudden change in your lifestyle if the media is alerted to a mistake or mishap. Imagine if you were Tiger Woods. As most recall from Thanksgiving weekend in 2009, Woods was pulling out of his driveway in Isleworth, a prestigious golf resort and gated luxury home community in Windermere (southwest Orlando), when his SUV hit a tree and a fire hydrant.

It took a few days to learn what precipitated the accident. It turns out Woods was sleeping around with multiple women, and when his wife found out, she went after him. Deceit had caught up to him.

What ensued afterward was a media circus. The press was camped out at the Isleworth gates for days. The road that passes in front of the resort is two lanes wide so people could literally drive by, reach out their window, and grab a microphone. The circus went on for three weeks until the Windermere Police Department kicked the media out of the area, citing safety concerns.

What would you do if that happened to you?

The best advice is to live an honest life. Don't cheat on your spouse or your steady. Don't steal. Don't deceive. You will eventually be found out, even for something you might consider minor. The media loves nothing more than a scandal. They love it even more if the scandal stretches out over several days, months, or years (as in Woods' case).

Consider what happened to Scott Thompson, the former CEO of Yahoo. He lied about his educational background on his resume. What's more, he tried to explain it away as a "little white lie." He claimed to have earned a computer science degree, which was not true. It took about two weeks for Yahoo to respond, and they let Thompson go.

That was two weeks too long. A story like that will play out in the media until there's a resolution. People in the news media have a job to do, and that is to tell a story no matter the consequences. If a company or individual allows a negative story to linger, the media will churn it until someone is arrested, fired, or resigns.

It's the same with a faulty product. A company may not want to issue a recall, but it may be forced into action due to public opinion or a government requirement. If you're in a situation where the media is clamoring for answers, it's best to face the truth right away and fix whatever problems exist. In most cases, waiting only makes things worse.

If you delay making an apology or admitting to a wrong, things can get out of hand. Recall what happened to former NFL running back O.J. Simpson, who had a marvelous career on the gridiron. After his playing days were over, he lost the structure of competing in a regimented sport and things eventually spun out of control.

In June 1994, Simpson's former wife and an acquaintance were found stabbed to death in an apartment in Los Angeles. The police department, suspecting Simpson had murdered the pair due to jealousy, set a time for the former sports star to turn himself in before the trial. The trouble was, Simpson never showed.

Later in the day, he was spotted in the passenger seat of a white Ford Bronco traveling down a Los Angeles-area freeway. Someone notified the authorities.

When the police cars got too close to the vehicle, the driver would yell that Simpson had a gun and would kill himself if the authorities didn't back off. The police continued to follow closely behind.

The chase went on for more than an hour. The media soon joined the action, and some 20 helicopters were in pursuit, each with one or two cameras and a reporter on board. All of the TV and cable stations at the time broke from their regular programming to cover the action — meaning millions and millions of people were watching live.  Given the limited technology, some of the newscasts were appearing on competing stations.

The white Bronco eventually arrived at Simpson's home. He remained in the vehicle for nearly an hour. During that time, his family negotiated with the police for more time. Simpson wanted to enter his home to speak with his mother. The police agreed. A short time later, his lawyer arrived and Simpson turned himself in to the authorities. When the trial concluded, Simpson was acquitted, although he faced multiple civil claims.

Today, Simpson sits in a jail cell, having been convicted of armed robbery and kidnapping in Las Vegas. It seems a group of individuals had stolen sports memorabilia from Simpson, and he decided to retrieve the items by breaking into a hotel room with a small group of men. Simpson received 33 years for the offenses, with the possibility of parole in 2017.

Had Simpson first turned himself in when required in 1994, the car chase would never have happened. Because of all of the publicity stirred up by the car chase, the resulting murder trial was a media circus, with headlines blaring, "The Trial of the Century." Indeed, it was. The subsequent trial over the sports memorabilia created a second media circus.

In all of your dealings with the media, the best advice is to hire a public relations expert to manage your interviews, press releases, statements, and other public disclosures. Don't delay like O.J. Simpson. It only makes matters worse. Face the media as soon as possible.

CHAPTER TWELVE

MEETING THAT CERTAIN PERSON

IT NEVER HURTS TO ARRIVE LIKE JAMES BOND. IF YOU'RE THE TALK OF THE PARTY, CHANCES ARE GOOD THAT YOU'LL BE INVITED BACK.

There's often a continental breakfast, networking session, or cocktail reception before a main event begins. At most important gatherings, there are one or several head tables. Before getting a drink, take a little time to scan the VIP reception and main room so you have a good idea of the layout.

Where will the key attendees be seated, and what is your seating position relative to them? If you're attempting to meet one or several business leaders or VIPs, often the best time is during the networking period or the VIP reception.

Most executives and leaders appear at VIP receptions, but not always. If it's a high-level person like Robert L. Johnson, Bill Gates, or Arianna Huffington, chances are they'll skip the meet-and-greet due to their schedule, or because they want to avoid a potentially embarrassing encounter (especially if their company made recent layoffs or a labor strike is under way).

If that key person isn't at the pre-event, it means he or she will enter the main room by a side door or from behind the podium. If that's the case, the only chance of meeting the person or getting a word in is to position yourself next to what is now the VIP's exit. If it's an event with a high-level speaker such as the president of the United States, you won't get near him or her unless you're a major campaign donor, trusted friend, or organizer of the event.

The Secret Service, or a company's security team, will have everything worked out ahead of time. That means the speaker will arrive from the rear of the building, perhaps through the kitchen or up a dedicated elevator.

When a high-level speaker is introduced, he or she will typically come from the side or the rear of the podium. They will almost always exit that way. In most instances, you will have no chance of personally meeting this person. But let all your contacts, friends, and associates know you were there via Facebook, Google+, Twitter, or any number of social apps.

If you really wanted to meet the VIP guest but were unable to, send the VIP a follow-up letter or e-mail. Learn about the person's future appearances by using a search engine or networking with their staff. You especially want to make friends with the executive assistant, as they often act as the gatekeeper. Perhaps the VIP will be speaking down the road at another event where you will be in attendance. Ask to meet them there, if they have the time. It's probably a long shot, but you'll never know if you don't try.

If you or your company are a friend or a major donor and were selected to mingle with or meet a VIP, prepare to have your picture taken. Ninety-nine times out of 100, a photographer will have been hired. Most often, you can bring a camera (not too large) or rely on your smart phone. Get a friend or acquaintance to take your photo.

The pictures always look good on the office wall or a mantle. One note of caution: If you display a large picture of President Obama in your office or home, be sure to consider who will see it. If you're attempting to land a major contract and the principal of the company supports Republicans, it may be a good idea to put the picture in a desk drawer or inside a closet during the meeting.

Overall, a small fame wall is always fun, and can typically lighten the stress for someone meeting you in your office for the first time. People will be impressed with the VIPs you've met, and it's a good conversation-starter. But don't overdo it. Too many photos on your fame wall can be creepy.

Evening sessions offer the most potential for meeting a VIP, as that's the last event of the day. But if a key person is visiting from out of town and their private jet is idling on a nearby tarmac, it makes things more difficult. That jet costs thousands of dollars per hour to operate, so move in quickly and subtly. Be efficient, and choose your words carefully.

Get to the point. Always introduce yourself by giving your name, your title, and company. Hand over your business card promptly. Don't be afraid to jump in with your request right away. Time is money, in this instance.

Whether it's a commercial airline, train, or boat, the guest of honor may have a ticket for the last departure of the day. As mentioned, setting and keeping a tight schedule in today's increasingly busy business world is paramount to success. Woody Allen had it right: "Eighty percent of success is showing up." The other 20 percent is sticking to a schedule, being prepared, and trusting your instincts if things veer off course.

If the VIP invites you to share the ride back to the airport, accept the offer. Either the VIP will make arrangements to have his or her driver take you back, or you can get a cab for the return trip. One-on-one time is the best of all. Just don't waste it talking about the time you broke your leg in the third grade or, worse, the weather. Get to the point. There's plenty of time to socialize after a business matter has been addressed and dealt with.

If you're attending an event for the first time and an Internet search fails to shed much light on things, call the venue to gather informa-  tion. A well-trained and seasoned receptionist, booking manager, or room planner can offer valuable assistance.

Let them know you may be running late, and ask what time they expect most guests to arrive. If you have food allergies, inquire into the menu or any served food or drinks (if the drinks are complimentary, it's a good indicator the event is upscale). If a particular organization hosts an event, say a nonprofit, call their offices and ask to speak with the main planner or assistant.

Consider being a sponsor or donating an item for a silent or live auction. Your name or your company's name, or both, will be mentioned or listed. What's more, the event chairs will be impressed and will help make key introductions for you.

The car companies and dealerships are incredible at this; they make sure to have their cars or trucks on display both at the entrance to an event and inside. Who doesn't want Lincoln or Cadillac as a major sponsor? It just raises the bar of the event and promotes ticket sales. Everyone wants to be part of a winning team.

Before you arrive, research the parking arrangements. Again, learn how the valet works at every given venue. You can park by yourself much more quickly, and while there may be a bit of a walk, at least you're moving and a quick exit is assured. In many facilities, especially a busy hotel or casino, it can take 10 minutes or longer to reach the valet. That doesn't seem like much time, but if you missed a key connection because you were waiting outside to check your car, it might as well be an eternity.

Such a strategy assumes you want to leave an event quickly. Upon departure, it can take even more time to retrieve a vehicle after you hand your ticket back to a valet or cashier. To boost your chances of arriving at an event without a hitch, research other entrance points. Many cities offer multiple modes of transportation — rail, bus, or boat docks. OK, a helicopter pad is the ultimate, but often it's not practical, and it's rather expensive. Still, what could be cooler than arriving by helicopter?

The only other thing that compares is a seaplane, predicated on the fact that the event is located next to, or near, a large body of water. Naturally, you must ensure your pilot has researched any air restrictions or municipal requirements before setting a seaplane in the water.

But keep in mind, most local officials — including the police, city workers, and county prosecutors — like to assert their authority. So when a seaplane flies into a particular area, albeit legally, ambitious and often ignorant officials like to make a scene. Having experienced such behavior firsthand, the education process falls in your lap and your pilot's lap.

Once a seaplane lands in an unrestricted body of water, it becomes a boat and is regulated as such, but so many local officials treat the unannounced arrival of a seaplane in a body of water as an affront to their authority. In one instance, a police officer showed up after our party landed in a seaplane and entered a private event. The pilot, who was an invited guest, spoke with the officer and informed him that it was perfectly legal to land in the bay. After checking the gentleman's pilot's license (which was up to date), the officer left.

Two weeks later, the pilot received a call from the prosecutor's office on a Saturday morning, informing him that a warrant had been issued for his arrest. Prosecutors like to call on weekends, when most people are presumed to be at home. The charges included flying too low, and careless and reckless flying.

Even after the pilot had the FAA call the prosecutor and explain that the charges were unfounded and superseded by federal law, the prosecutor refused to budge. After a fairly stressful and somewhat expensive period of time, the charges were dropped. As it stood, the prosecutor saw an opportunity to get some positive media coverage to improve his standing in the community as an aggressive public safety official. Too bad the plan backfired. As it turns out, the press was fairly negative and focused on the prosecutor's waste of tax revenue in the matter.

Let's take a quick diversion here, which is justified as it relates to working or interacting with public officials. A politician or public official's worst fear, apart from unforeseen accidents and threats to public safety, is bad press. After all, many public officials have large egos and if the public loses faith in their ability to lead, it makes any re-election or future position in public office that much more difficult to obtain.

To avoid or limit such encounters, do your homework. In the case of the pilot, he made sure the FAA was aware of his flight plan. It also doesn't hurt to let local and county police know of your arrival and departure, as well as the security team at the facility you are visiting. A good communication plan helps everyone and, in most instances, your pilot can see to all the necessary arrangements.

Pack an overnight bag just in case bad weather moves in. Make a reservation at a nearby hotel. It doesn't cost anything to cancel the room, provided you remember.

So why go to all this trouble? It never hurts to arrive like James Bond. If you're the talk of the party, chances are good you'll be invited back. At the next event, you'll have an easier time securing a more strategically advantageous table. But don't get carried away. No one likes an aloof person who brags about cars or jewelry. Stay humble. Make an entrance, but don't overdo it.

As you prepare to meet a VIP, keep in mind a keynote speaker or honoree will likely be focused on their upcoming remarks, especially if it's a difficult program with a lot of moving parts (if the main address is followed by a live auction, for instance).

Many people have no problem delivering a speech, while others avoid it until it becomes necessary. To discern the mood of the speaker before making an introduction (it's even better to be introduced by a business colleague or mutual friend), determine if the company's PR team or the speaker's family or friends are standing close by.

If it's the PR team, be forewarned. They are often there to run interference. Or they may be focused on impressing the boss, so they won't take kindly to a new visitor. On the latter point, don't let that stop you from introducing yourself to the guest of honor. The PR person may be upset, but if the VIP likes you, there's little they can do. After all, the PR person doesn't want to make a scene and diminish their value in front of the boss.

If the speaker is standing with his or her family and everyone is huddled close

MEETING THAT CERTAIN VIP:

MAKE NOTE OF ENTRY/ EXIT POINTS

CHECK POSITION OF HEAD TABLE EARLY ON

SPEAKER WILL BE MORE RELAXED AFTER EVENT

MAKE YOUR INTRODUC- TION, GET TO THE POINT

DON'T INTERRUPT OR BREAK UP A CON- VERSATION

together, it means the speaker is likely stressing about the speech, doesn't feel like mingling, or is feeling insecure.

An outgoing VIP will circulate throughout the room, no problem. Keep an eye out as you mingle, and look for a window of opportunity to introduce yourself (and remember the buddy system).

Short of that, a good back-up plan is to make your introduction after the salad is served and before the main course arrives (or between dinner and dessert). There's always a lull between courses. To execute an introduction between servings, you need to determine where the main speaker is seated, and whether he or she is engaged in a deep conservation.

Timing is everything in this instance. If other people at the speaker's table are talking amongst themselves, or are too intimidated by the speaker, chances are good you can get in and out with a well-crafted and engaging greeting. Have a business card or two ready to go. You don't want to be fumbling for your business card holder at a time like this, unless it's incredibly distinctive and can be accessed quickly. Keep a couple of cards loose in your pocket or purse. Easy access is key.

Not every introduction works the first time, but at least you have set the stage for the next encounter ("Nancy, nice to see you again. Wasn't that a great fundraiser the United Way put on last month at the Marriott?"). Effective recollection is your friend in such a greeting, especially if you see the VIP randomly. Now that you've gotten their undivided attention, move in for the request. Sometimes it's that simple.

If, at the first encounter, the VIP starts looking around aimlessly, or is intent on meeting or calling someone over, get in and out quickly. There's nothing worse than when a newcomer to a conversation goes on and on about a particular topic, like what part of Italy their shoes came from. Unless the VIP is fully engaged, shake their hand and pull in close.

Ask your question(s) and find out the best way to follow up. Can you call, e-mail, or link through social media? The encounter will likely take two minutes or less, so maximize the rest of your time by networking.

When you're at a cocktail party, work the room. Always be mindful of the circle of conversation. If you are speaking to another person, leave a little room for someone else to enter the conversation (unless you want to monopolize the person's time).

As other people enter the conversation, keep everyone in a circle. If you feel someone on your right is looking to enter the group, step ever so slightly to your left or right, allow the person to enter the conversation, and reform the circle. But stay tight and stay engaged. You don't want the group forming into separate circles, as you could be the odd person out.

If the person on the right of you suddenly engages someone to his or her right, and the person on your left is speaking with someone else, you are left speaking to no one. That looks bad. To counteract this, you can either reform the circle with the person on your left or right, or bow out graciously. Look for someone else to meet, or take the opportunity to order a drink or use the bathroom.

Sometimes you can look to break the circle. If you see a key executive speaking with a couple, it's usually no problem entering the circle. Wait for a break in the conversation and introduce yourself. In most instances, you will have a few minutes as the couple either runs out of questions or is eager to follow a new conversation.

What should you say? Inquire about how things are going, or recall a recent accomplishment by the VIP or the hosting organization. Keep the VIP engaged as you delve into the efficiency of their new production line or their strategy to counteract rising commodity values, dollar swings, or foreign trade patterns.

Prepare and practice your greeting ahead of time until it becomes old hat. A well-polished greeting can go a long way, and you can also entertain other people — in this case, the couple standing with the VIP.

Control your future and that of your guests. Scan the room for the nearest bathrooms, the bar, and the trash or recycling receptacles. When required, you can be the consummate guest by pointing out the location of various activities to others. Be indispensable. Before heading to the bar for another drink, ask everyone else in your party if they need anything. It's the proper thing to do.

Over time, you will get to know numerous people. But sometimes there are those events where even the most active socializer knows only one or two people, or perhaps no one.

In this instance, just introduce yourself and say you're new to the area or to the particular group hosting the party. Ask your new friend(s) to show you around, point out certain people, or make introductions. Most people will be happy to make introductions if they aren't actively engaged with a duty, such as making sure to close the silent auction.

Don't leave right after dinner unless you really have someplace to be. See if there is an afterglow, and determine whether your intended person of opportunity will be attending. This is when the VIP will be most relaxed. The main event is over, and it's time to have fun.

But don't rely on this; keep it as a fallback, especially if the VIP is with a spouse or significant other. A spouse or a partner of the VIP has needs, and they've likely been very patient leading up to this moment. After all, a speech takes time to prepare and rehearse. And during the event, the spouse patiently waits as his or her VIP partner works the room or is sought after. He or she may be looking forward to dancing afterward.

When it's time to leave, don't take more than one parting gift unless the host or event organizer encourages you to take one or two extra items. If it's a key client or supplier, take the gift(s). No sense offending them. Display the item in your office. People love that.

After successfully navigating an event and meeting your key targets, don't get greedy at the end. If it's a valued gift, like a replica scale model of a 1953 Chevrolet Corvette, by all means take one. If it's your basic swag — monogrammed pens, notepads, hats, or shirts — best to leave it unless you run the risk of offending your host. After all, how many monogrammed pens do you need?

Remember, you're always representing the company or organization. You want to be the best guest possible. Don't make a scene. Play the part of a good guest, work the room, have fun, and add value.

13 LUNCH IS SERVED!

IF YOUR GUEST SEASONS A DISH BEFORE TASTING IT, IT'S LIKELY HE OR SHE MAKES ASSUMPTIONS BEFORE KNOWING THE WHOLE STORY.

Lunch is my favorite meal of the day. Yes, breakfast and dinner are great, but lunch is the most productive. People tend to be at the top of their game at lunch. Typically, there's no drinking involved. At breakfast, most people are still waking up and getting into their routine. At dinner, the day is winding down, and people are getting tired. With wine or drinks flowing, it's hard to be at the top of your game.

Since I'm in the business of gathering information and assembling it into feature articles, there are times when I will have two or three lunches in a day. Why? It can take weeks to get on the schedule of a prominent business leader. Thankfully, I have the time to wait — especially if there's the potential for a great story.

There are days when the convergence of two lunches can't be helped. Naturally, you schedule them so you arrive on time for each. Be sure to eat light, perhaps soup and a small salad at the first lunch, and a plate of tuna salad and fruit at the other. Don't wolf down burgers back to back; it's bad for your health and you'll be falling asleep by mid-afternoon.

As with any meal where you're meeting someone for the first time, pay attention to the mannerisms of your guest. Are they fidgety, nervous, or callous? Read their eyes. Did they look you directly in the eye during the initial handshake? If they did, relax.

The person who looks others in the eye is often grounded, has a well-rounded education, and has likely traveled and mingled extensively among other cultures.

Does the person place their napkin on their lap right away? If the silverware is rolled up inside the napkin, study to see how they unfold the napkin and set the fork(s), knife(s), and spoon(s) in their proper position.

If they scatter the silverware, it typically means they are abstract, prone to untidiness (although they likely know where everything is), and can meet a deadline, but it may be a mad scramble to get there.

If they arrange the silverware perfectly, you have a linear mind before you. This is someone who is neat, tidy, and to the point. They can plan well, meet goals, and typically operate successfully in a team environment. The worry here is that they're so linear that they lack the ability to dream. They rarely come up with creative solutions, or they don't adapt well to change.

In today's business climate, with so much information bombarding us, change is inevitable. If you're looking for a great engineer, chief financial officer, or department head, start with someone who is linear. They'll get the job done. The need for creativity, while always welcome, isn't a prerequisite to success. If they do come up with a great idea that saves you or the company time and money, consider it a bonus.

Nonlinear people are often great at product development — the lifeblood of most organizations — as well as design, architecture, advertising, or product launches. A great leader will recognize the need for linear and nonlinear people within their organization. Linear people can oversee a research and development team as long as they encourage creativity. Creative people go where they're most respected — meaning there's a hands-off environment coupled with state-of-the-art resources such as a fully equipped laboratory or design studio.

When linear people believe they know everything and begin to dictate design to meet their needs, problems are not far off. Much of what caused trouble for GM, Ford, and Chrysler in the late 1990s was that the linear people at the top dictated how cars and trucks should be designed. They wanted the fewest problems on the factory floor, so they streamlined everything. What sequences out at the other end may have been the cheapest product possible, but it's all for naught if people don't buy it.

Once the Big Three automakers learned to let their designers design, their collective fortunes turned for the better. It's the same in any arena. Apple struggled mightily in the 1990s until Steve Jobs returned in 1997 and set the company up for a masterful stroke of creativity — the iPod, iPhone, and iPad — along with allowing outsiders to add applications.

On the other hand, BlackBerry once held a commanding position in the smart phone sector, but sales began to languish because they lost their edge in design and creativity.

Once you've surveyed your guest's mannerisms, study how they order their lunch. Are they kind to the waiter, do they ask a lot of questions about the menu, or are they callous and rude? Taskmasters are no fun and, if they're not careful (and they often aren't), they can drive away the creative people.

Yes, taskmasters are needed to help people meet goals, but avoid rude and obnoxious people. I've seen it time and again. The taskmaster gets the CEO job and the board of directors begins to relax, thinking they have a steady driver at the wheel. But in six months to a year, chaos takes hold. People are jumping off the bus, the product developers leave for more open environments, and sales begin to slide.

When you sit down for lunch, present your business card early on. If the person doesn't bother to look at your card and shoves it in their pocket right away, your internal red flag should start to climb.

This is not an open-minded person. They likely have a big ego. Do you want to do business with them if they can't show a small degree of courtesy? The answer is probably no.

PLAYING THE HOST:

IF YOU INVITE SOMEONE TO DINE, PAY FOR THE MEAL

IF TIME IS AN ISSUE, PREORDER FOOD OR GO BUFFET

OVERSEE MOST INTERACTIONS WITH WAIT STAFF

CALL AHEAD WITH ANY SPECIAL REQUESTS

PREPARE AN AGENDA AND SHARE IT

While you're minding table mannerisms, be sure to keep an eye out for the waiter. Introduce your guest and yourself (in that order) right away. What other tables do they have? Is the waiter responsive to a change on the menu? Do they have your back?

The last thing you want is a waiter who disappears for long stretches of time. Remember, you are always acting like the host. Yes, the waiter may have too many diners that day, but you're on a schedule.

If the waiter is slow, ask a fellow waiter, a server, or a maître d' to intercede. Sometimes you have to take charge. Ask them to find your waiter or write up a bill. Remember, the entire staff is dedicated to serving the guests.

I almost always tip 20 percent, even though the standard is 15 percent to 18 percent. I will tip 25 percent, or even 30 percent, if the service and food was extraordinary. A larger tip also is warranted if you closed the big deal or your guests(s) had an exceptional time. For more information on tipping, please visit the Corporate Resource Guide on Page 110.

If you return to a restaurant or club often, there's a good chance you'll receive excellent service. Believe me, waiters will be falling over themselves to serve you if you provide generous tips. They all know the game. But they have to earn it. Make sure they do. You're driving the results.

As for reservations, check in with the restaurant beforehand to secure an excellent table or a fine waiter. Call during slow hours. Don't call during breakfast, lunch, or dinner, when the restaurant is at its busiest. Call a few weeks ahead of time for a reservation, especially if it's a popular establishment.

After you've ordered, it's best to get to the business at hand. Learn to be a good small-talker. You want your guest to be comfortable, and most people are very comfortable talking about themselves. But be mindful of the direction and scope of the conversation. Don't offer up too many personal questions, for fear of putting your guest on edge. You want to ask simple questions, like where they were raised, how they reached their particular position, or even where they like to vacation.

Begin to get to the point. Have an agenda set ahead of time. If you'd like to write it down as an outline and have a copy for the other person, that's fine. Be sure to leave room for notes. Follow up quickly on any requests, such as an e-mail they may be interested in, or a report, or a referral. If it's a referral, be sure to copy that person on the e-mail so your guest can make an easy connection.

I like to bring my iPad to lunch. That way, if a guest mentions a website, I can look it up right away. You can send e-mails on the spot. The ability to view and make decisions using an iPad is invaluable, and makes for a much richer and deeper experience. Plus, you don't have to follow up afterward, other than with a thank-you note.

As the waiter returns with an appetizer or entrée, watch your guest's mannerisms. Do they hold the fork and knife correctly? Are they sloppy eaters? Do they stab at their food? Do they chew with their mouth open? My friend Sara makes a good point: If your guest seasons a dish before tasting it, it's likely he or she makes assumptions before knowing the whole story.

If the waiter brings something from the kitchen that has not been prepared right, consider your time. It may take another 15 minutes for the dish to be prepared again. You may have time at dinner to wait, given the next stop is home.

But at breakfast or lunch, with your schedule to maintain, you often don't have time to wait.

When the check arrives, the general rule is the person who called for the lunch should pay for the lunch. To ensure you will be the one responsible for the check, arrange payment with the restaurant ahead of time. Or excuse yourself, track down the waiter, and hand over your credit card.

Be on guard. If a restaurant caters your company's events and they do a poor job at your lunch, you may want to change operators. When you see a restaurant cheap out on the food, it's best never to come back. Don't give them more business or hire them as a caterer if they're not performing to your expectations.

You don't want your clients or employees eating inconsistently prepared food. Your events should sparkle and be memorable. Your guests should be raving about the food, the level of service, and the presentation. Unless you can host an event that hits those three points, it's not worth doing.

Find a restaurant or caterer you trust, and stay with them. If you don't know of one, ask your most trusted friends. The last thing you want is a business deal to go sour because you decided to save money on the food or your supposed friend, the caterer, slips up.

So what happens if the food is bad at an event you hosted? What appeared to be a good meal turns out to be a disaster the following day; your guest(s) got sick due to food poisoning. If that happens, they most likely will call your office to complain.

After the first person calls with a complaint, put your receptionist on alert, as well as any staff members who attended the party (if they aren't sick, as well). Let your guests know how sorry you are and refer them to the restaurant or caterer. One or two sick calls may not be enough to point the finger at the food preparers. But if you are fielding multiple calls, chances are very good that the restaurant or caterer is to blame.

If the dining operator has any class, they'll offer gift certificates, although most people won't accept them. Barring that, it's best to apologize profusely. If the restaurant won't do anything, send each sick person a nice bottle of wine or some other small gift.

We once hosted a party at a restaurant and half the crowd got sick. Following a review by the health department, it was discovered that the cooking staff allowed the chicken to thaw too long. In turn, they didn't cook the stuffed chicken breasts properly. The affected guests weren't happy campers and they either called our office, the restaurant, the health department, or the media to complain.

In some cases, they called everyone. If the media does call, refer them to the restaurant. If they ask for a response to a story about diners getting sick, refer them again to the restaurant. Do not answer any more questions.

If you own the restaurant and the media calls asking about tainted food being served, have a statement prepared for release. A reporter assigned to the story will keep digging if you provide no comment. Apologize and take the high road. The statement should relay that a problem occurred in the handling and preparation of the food, and that steps have been taken to ensure it will never happen again. If it wasn't an isolated incident, chances are your restaurant will be out of business in quick order, either due to a lack of patrons or pressure from the health department.

If you choose not to comment to the media, you can believe the reporter will be interviewing the health department, affected guests, your competition, and restaurant experts. More aggressive reporters, especially television reporters, may arrive for an unscheduled interview in hopes of extracting an ill-advised comment from you.

If you have a statement prepared soon after the incident, you can read from it. The reporter may try to follow you and stick a microphone in your face, but just keep walking and stick to the script: "Please see our statement."

While the vast majority of people want to do a good job, accidents do happen. To prepare for any fallout, hire a public relations and marketing firm to develop an emergency disaster plan for your company or organization. Hopefully, it will never be needed. But if an accident does occur, it's best to be prepared.

A good disaster plan will detail how to respond to a crisis such as food poisoning or an explosion. There will be time to figure out what caused the accident, which 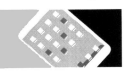 could take months, but you need a plan to deal with the short-term fallout. What public safety agencies need to be called, how will the plant or business be evacuated, and what insurance is needed to care for everyone affected? This is not an area you want to leave to chance. Be prepared for the worst.

Getting back to your lunch partner, be the consummate host, be mindful of and learn from your guest's mannerisms, and attend to all of their needs, including arrival and departure. In addition, alert your guest(s) to any rules right away. Many private clubs, for example, have a dress code, or they only allow people to talk on smart phones in dedicated areas. Follow and share the rules. You don't want to make a scene or, worse, put your guest in a bad light.

14 ON THE ROAD

REMEMBER, CRIMINALS OFTEN WORK IN PAIRS. BE MINDFUL THAT ONE BUMP AGAINST A POCKET OR JACKET MAY BE RAPIDLY FOLLOWED BY ANOTHER.

The last thing you need is to be taken for a joyride.

When you're hiring a driver, take a few precautions. Look the driver in the eyes and trust your sixth sense. Did you get a good vibe or a bad vibe?

If you felt a bad vibe, or are concerned in any way about your safety, tell the driver to wait 10 seconds before moving and let them know you're pinning your location and sending it to your assistant (or a family member or friend).

They won't ask why, but it does put them on notice that you are not alone.

Is the driver's operating permit displayed on the passenger side of the dashboard? If not, ask the driver where it is. If he or she doesn't have a permit, they likely don't have a driver's license. If you're traveling in America and running late for a meeting or appointment, trust your instincts. If you're in a foreign country, find another cab, regardless.

Sometimes a taxi driver shows up drunk or buzzed from marijuana or some other drug. The eyes are a dead giveaway. Are the eyes bloodshot, droopy, or lazy? If the driver slurs his or her speech, call and ask for another driver. And report the condition of the driver. Yes, you will lose time, but your safety won't be compromised.

What is the condition of the cab interior? If it's clean and tidy, you can rest a little easier. Always wear a safety belt, whether it's a cab, a company car, a rental vehicle, a luxury sedan, a limousine, or a plane.

Need proof?

Following the Detroit Red Wings' Stanley Cup victory in June 1997, star defenseman Vladimir Konstantinov and two of his friends hired a limousine. The driver, who had a suspended license (drunk driving), fell asleep at the wheel and smashed into a tree. Unfortunately, no one was wearing a seatbelt.

Konstantinov and another passenger sustained severe injuries from the crash. The star hockey player never dressed for another game. His career was over in less than five seconds. Had the passengers been wearing seatbelts, it's likely all three of them would have escaped the crash with minor injuries.

As a general rule, a luxury sedan service or limousine operator has better drivers than cab companies, but never let your guard down. Check to see if the transportation company has a good safety record. Search on Google for any safety violations or other suspicious activity.

When the car pulls away from the curb, be sure you're headed in the right direction, and don't be shy about providing turn-by-turn navigation. Follow along on your phone if you're not familiar with a particular area.

Cab drivers, who charge by the mile, have been known to take the long way. Yes, they may know about high traffic volumes in certain areas, especially around rush hour, so trust them to an extent.

If the ride was uneventful, a nice tip is in order. Typically it's 15 percent for shorter rides and 20 percent for longer rides. If the driver helps with your bag or opens the door for you, a larger tip is in order. It's the same with luxury sedan drivers and chauffeurs. If they are attentive and courteous, go with 20 percent. If not, drop it down to 15 percent or whatever you're comfortable with.

If possible, travel with several bill denominations. Some drivers don't like to break large bills. The cab driver may accept a credit or a debit card, as well. Don't be shy about asking for a receipt. Most companies require receipts for any reimbursement on an expense account.

If the driver balks, write the day and time of the cab ride, the mileage, and any pertinent information like the driver's name, cab car number, driver permit number, and the license plate. Another idea is to take a picture while you're in the cab so you can jot it down later.

Never cheat on your expense report. If you get caught, chances are you'll be reprimanded or fired. Use the IRS mileage rate unless your company has a set policy.

If you're traveling alone in a foreign country, a larger company may hire a driver/

security team for your protection. Even if you work for a smaller company, ask about a security detail. A trusted security team is an absolute must when traveling in Third World countries. As noted, foreign criminals, cartels, gangs, and drug lords target American executives, so be sure to read up on the political scene of a given country before your business trip.

As a general rule, plan your trip around political or religious demonstrations. Call the U.S. Embassy in a given country for an update on security precautions. Be sure to memorize the address and note the embassy's location relative to other buildings or monuments. It will come in handy in case you lose your smart phone or the battery fades. Some smart phones may not even work.

In the days leading up to an election, an unscrupulous foreign political leader may show off their mettle to the electorate by capturing a visiting U.S. business-person. Because of this security risk, most companies have strict policies about traveling to, say, Venezuela or Argentina during an election season. They don't want the private jet seized on the tarmac or a luxury sedan commandeered by criminals loyal to the present regime.

Keep from announcing or telegraphing your travel plans. If an organization seeks to honor you, be sure the group is legitimate. There are plenty of stories where American executives or professional athletes have become unwitting kid-napping targets because they agreed to be at a certain place at a certain time. In most instances, a corporate security team will weigh in on where and when you can travel.

If you're traveling in a Third World country, don't set your meetings until you're on the ground. Again, it keeps people guessing where you might be. Don't venture out alone, especially at night. Stay in your hotel or a guest home.

Do your homework.

Picking the right hotel can be a challenge. If your company has an account with a certain hotel chain, trust that the accommodations have been screened. In addi-tion, check to see if the hotel has been the target of kidnappers or terrorists. The nicer the hotel, the more likely criminals will target it.

Recall that a group of Islamic terrorists from Pakistan attacked close to a dozen tourist and civic facilities in Mumbai, India, in late November 2008. Among the targets were luxury hotels, a hospital, a Jewish center, and a cinema. Since there was no advanced warning, it was impossible to prepare for the attack. It took sev-eral days to restore order, and in the end 164 people were killed while another 308 people were injured.

While there isn't much anyone can do to completely avoid a terrorist attack, be on guard at all times while on the road. Leave most, if not all, of your jewelry at home.

Thieves look for easy targets, so dress conservatively. Buy decent, but not expensive, suitcases, and be mindful of pulling lots of currency from your pocket or purse.

I recommend a simple money clip and a small leather case to carry two credit cards and a money card. It also doubles as a business card holder. I keep it in a front pocket, as it's much more difficult for a pickpocket to steal something there. Plus, you can have your hands in your pocket for added safety. Keep your passport and smart phone there, as well.

If your passport is stolen or lost, call the local embassy. Before you travel, jot down your passport number and other important information, like the expiration date, on a small card and keep it with you. Keep a paper copy of your passport in another pocket or elsewhere on your person. Take a photo of your passport with your smart phone, as well.

Another idea is to list your passport information under contacts in your phone, tablet, or other electronic device. Put it under a fake name as an extra measure of safety. It will go a long way toward helping you out should you need to obtain another passport.

Always lock your phone, tablet, or laptop. Be sure to sign up for a service that can locate an electronic device in case it is misplaced, lost, or stolen. Learn how to wipe out your smart phone remotely, as a precaution in the event it is stolen. You don't want your information in the hands of a criminal.

Carrying a large wallet or cell phone in a back pocket or inside a suit coat or a jacket is a crime waiting to happen. It's the same for a small purse with thin straps. Be sure to select a conservative suitcase or leather bag with strong straps. Leave your Louis Vuitton or Chanel purse or handbag at home when traveling on business. Gentlemen should follow the same rule — no designer suitcases.

But don't go overboard. A metal suitcase with impressive locks may come in handy, but remember a thief will take note. People who wear expensive clothing and jewelry or flash a lot of cash are easy marks for thieves. Plus, your host and

DID YOU KNOW...

FLYING PRIVATE:

1. ARRIVE WITH PLENTY OF TIME TO SPARE

2. EAT AND DRINK SPARINGLY

3. BRING A SHARED GIFT (CHAMPAGNE/STRAWBERRIES)

4. DO NOT TALK IN A LOUD VOICE

5. AVOID ALL JOKES ABOUT HIJACKERS/TERRORISTS

potential new business contact will think you charge too much for your services or products if you are dressed to the nines. Save the jewelry for the home front.

Once you've checked into a hotel, be sure to study the layout. Identify all of the exits and take a walk to identify where they are located. Remember to take all of your valuables with you, including any laptop computers, tablets, cell phones, and other devices.

Hotel rooms are extremely easy to break into. Be sure to check the locks on your room door, as well as those on all of the windows. Consider bringing your own door lock. There are many secure, simple-to-use locks on the market.

It doesn't take much for a thief to climb up a downspout of a multistory building, or they can traverse from the roof. A balcony or window ledge offers another entry point for criminals, so be sure to test all of the locks.

If you plan to lock items in a hotel room safe, make sure it is bolted securely to the floor or a wall. If possible, change the combination of the lock right away. If the lock has a key, be sure to keep the key with you at all times, including in the shower. Thieves will break into a room if they know someone is in the shower.

Lock the door when you're in the bathroom, even if you are alone. Be sure to have your phone in case someone enters your room. Call the front desk immediately. Some bathrooms have phones, as well.

When entering a hotel room for the first time, check for anyone or anything under the bed. I have never found a human or an animal under a bed, but you never know. Make sure the bellhop is present as you search the room, or multiple rooms.

For added security, consider carrying a small, shrill siren or a laser pointer. Mace or pepper spray also works, but commercial airlines don't allow them on board, especially on international flights.

Still, they're available at most airports or drug stores. Keep any medications with you at all times, and ask at the front desk where the nearest major medical facility is located. If you are injured in a foreign land, have a doctor provide basic treatment. Leave the specialized work for your return. The U.S. health care system is the best in the world, which is why so many foreign students attend medical school in the United States.

If you need to exchange currency in a foreign country, be as discreet as possible. Enter and leave a bank or financial institution with your money, traveler's checks, or credit cards in a secure place, preferably deep inside a front pants pocket.

Trust no one.

I recall walking out of a currency exchange center near the Paris Opera House.

It was very crowded on the sidewalk. An elderly woman reached into my back pocket, but there was nothing there. Since there were too many people around to make a scene — and assuming she wasn't alone — I kept walking.

Had she come away empty-handed and started screaming, I was prepared to scream with her. If this happens, scream at the top of your voice and call the person out. Call them a thief, and let everyone know there was a potential robbery.

If they proceed to call for the police, do the same thing. Match them step for step. Often, the police will believe the first person that calls in a potential crime.

Remember, criminals can work in pairs. Be mindful that one bump against a pocket or jacket may be rapidly followed by another.

If possible, don't use a cell phone while you're walking in a large crowd or in tight quarters. If you do need to use your phone in a crowded space, keep looking from side to side as you walk, and stop occasionally to see if you're being followed.

If someone is following you, slip into a restaurant, a store, or any public place. What's more, take note of the nearest security desk or police station as you move from district to district or city to city. It's always better to be safe than sorry.

The old adage "don't talk to strangers" is great advice. If someone you don't know approaches and strikes up a conversation, provide brief, yet general responses. Whenever I get a bad vibe about a stranger, I go into alternative reality mode. I always say that I work as a janitor back home. I tell people I come from a long line of janitors, and that our family has been cleaning office buildings for more than a century.

Talking about unpleasant duties like cleaning a toilet is never fun, but it works wonders when you're trying to deflect suspicious queries. Never give details about your professional or personal lifestyle, unless it's general facts like you live in a modest house with two bedrooms and a small backyard. Let everyone believe you live a humble life.

At commercial airports, stay on alert. While security measures have greatly improved, keep in mind that most foreign airports aren't as safe as those in the United States. Pack all of your valuables in a conservative carry-on bag, along with an extra set of clothes. It's a great back-up in case the airport or airline loses your checked bags (the contents of which should be easily replaceable).

Be mindful if anyone follows you into a restroom. Bring all of your belongings into a stall. Hang things on a hook, if possible. A thief can easily reach down and grab a bag on the floor, especially when you're going about your business.

If you're traveling on a cruise ship or on an overnight train, take all of the previously mentioned precautions. Hopefully, you have a private cabin suite. If not, make sure to put all of your valuables in a safe. Short of that, you'll need to bring all of your valuables with you, including to the dining car and the bathroom. Again, a screwdriver is often all a thief needs to force his or her way into an empty room.

The last thing you need to lose is a laptop computer, tablet, or smart phone. With iCloud and other services, most data is easily backed up, but you certainly don't want to allow a thief or a rival company to get their hands on your company's revolutionary new product or expansion plans. Apart from losing any key data, you could be fired for being so careless.

Consider buying traveler's insurance and traveler's checks. The vast majority of credit card companies offer such services. When I'm traveling, I prefer to pay for expenses on a credit card. And I always make sure to carry two different cards. Most often, credit card companies such as American Express offer reasonable and fair exchange rates, and they provide an organized statement.

Save all of your receipts and be sure to match them with what's on your statement. Most credit card companies will cancel and re-issue a card if there are unauthorized charges. If your card is lost or stolen, it can be easily be wiped clean and replaced with a new one. Ask your credit card company to provide a security question before canceling a card. That way, no one can call and cancel your card.

As a back-up, visit your bank or credit union before a business trip. You may need foreign currency to pay cab drivers or provide tips to hotel employees. Whatever currency you have left over can easily be exchanged back home.

Don't hold or carry anything for a stranger. If someone asks you to watch or hold a package, most likely it's a scam. It's better to be rude and decline any such invitation. You don't need to be the unsuspecting victim of a possible crime in a foreign country.

Don't pick up an item, either. If someone offers a key and asks you to retrieve a bag or something else from a locker, decline the invitation. A person can come up with what seems like a rational explanation for having a stranger pick up a bag, but don't get involved. You have no idea what's in the locker, and it could be that the police or other criminals are monitoring the area.

The locker may house stolen jewels, drugs, or a bomb. Let them get their own bag.

Don't be fooled by people with apparent hardships, such as someone in a wheelchair or an arm cast. It could easily be a ruse. By playing up a supposed hardship, the thief is hoping you'll let your guard down. Don't go for it. If someone needs help, direct him or her to the nearest security person or transportation employee.

Be mindful of what you eat. Make sure everything is cooked thoroughly. If you are at all concerned about the quality of the water, drink bottled water. Be sure the cap is securely fastened. Make sure to listen for the sound of air rushing in after you open a bottle or can.

There are plenty of stories out there of restaurant workers refilling bottles with tap water before tightening the caps. Consider drinking soda or fruit drinks from a sealed can.

Avoid ordering cold dishes such as salads. The lettuce and other vegetables were likely washed in unclean tap water. Also, avoid any ice. It's likely frozen unclean tap water.

The last thing you want on a business trip is a bout of food poisoning. If need be, eat sealed energy bars or other nutritional products. Whether at home or on the road, I always wipe my silverware with a napkin. You'd be surprised how often dishwater spots or specks of food can be found. Make sure the wine glass is free of spots, lipstick marks, or streaks.

Before you sit down for a meal, wash your hands. During a cocktail party you've likely greeted plenty of people, so be sure to wash your hands with hot water and soap.

Avoid touching your mouth, nose, or eyes with your fingers. Use a napkin — or, if you absolutely must, a sleeve — if you need to scratch your nose. A gentleman or lady should always carry a handkerchief or two. If someone coughs or sneezes in your direction, step back, turn away, or kneel down to adjust a shoe or lace. Avoid breathing for 10 seconds, to keep from inhaling germs.

When people stand too close and are talking directly to you, learn to turn your head slightly and breathe in. This is a great trick for people with bad breath. It can be difficult to comprehend a conversation when you're focused on your breathing, but it beats the alternative.

If someone you are speaking with has bad breath, it's better to endure the odor than call them out. If you do make mention of it, make sure it's in a soft, unassuming tone. If they become offended, don't worry about it. You did the right thing. Just don't yell it out to everyone.

One way to rectify the problem is to excuse yourself and make mention of the fact that you're headed to the bathroom for some mouthwash. Hopefully, the other person will get the hint. Short of mouthwash, be sure to carry gum or mints. Use them yourself, and be sure to invite other people to take one.

What happens if you have just eaten a piece of shrimp and your boss walks by and strikes up a conversation? Grab a napkin right away and hold it in front of your mouth as you speak. If a napkin is not readily available, hold a hand in front of your mouth. At the first opportunity, head to the bathroom and clean up. If there's no mouthwash and you don't have gum or mints handy, wash your hands and then rinse your mouth out with water. Use a hand to scoop water into your mouth, put a little soap on your index finger, and rub your teeth. Be sure to wipe your lips with a moist towel, as well. (In addition to freshening your breath, soap can remove tough stains like red wine.)

Another way to avoid bad breath after eating something is to speak without breathing out. Your voice won't be as robust, but at least you're not spreading a bad odor. A different approach is to hold a glass in front of your mouth as you speak. Pretend you are taking in the aroma of the wine, or take little sips of the liquid and breathe inside your glass. It also offers protection against someone else's bad breath.

On an airplane or in other tight quarters, the ability to catch or spread germs intensifies. When someone nearby coughs or sneezes, breathe in and out of a handkerchief. If you need to rub your mouth, nose, or eyes, use a handkerchief, a napkin, or a sleeve.

As you settle into a commercial flight, be sure to keep the other passengers within your view. Look for any suspicious behavior and report it immediately to a flight attendant. It could all be a misunderstanding, but you never know.

Never leave valuables in a rental car, including the trunk. A thief can wedge a thin strip of metal like a hanger through the driver's side window, hit the trunk button, and grab anything of value. In most cases, a car alarm won't be triggered.

I always get rental car insurance. It's not that much money and, if there is a problem, you're not left wondering if your own insurance will cover any damages (or the deductible). Before pulling out of a rental car parking space, walk around and inspect the vehicle for any damage. Of the several dozen cars I've rented over the years, I've found exterior dents on two separate occasions. You need to alert the clerk at the desk of any damage. Take pictures to avoid responsibility for pre-existing conditions.

Over the years, I've driven on various test tracks, often with a professional driver. Here are some of their tips: Always look ahead, but check your rearview mirror from time to time for police vehicles, speeding motorists, trucks that lose their brakes, or weaving motorcyclists. On wet pavement, take it easy, especially right after it starts to rain. The early rain mixes with surface oil, so the road will be slicker.

If you're driving on a freeway in the rain, use the center lane (which is slightly higher, to improve drainage). Avoid the freeways when it's snowing hard. It's often safer and less crowded on surface streets.

On dry pavement, ease your foot off the gas pedal going into a turn. Halfway through the turn, begin to accelerate slowly. It improves traction. Try to turn once rather than over-steer through a turn. Again, it improves traction. Get a hands-free phone system such as Ford's Sync offering. It's much easier than holding a phone. Don't multitask when driving. The human brain is equipped to concentrate on one or two things at a time.

Give trucks the right of way. A fully loaded 18-wheeler takes a long time to slow down. Don't tailgate, and don't get behind a truck or another vehicle that has a tarp. A friend of mine was behind a truck when the tarp flew off and covered her car. Fortunately, she was in the right lane. She hit the brakes and turned ever so slightly to the right so that she came to rest on the shoulder. Don't drive next to a truck, as its tires will kick up rocks and stones with more force than a smaller vehicle. Trucks also have a wider turning radius.

If you're pulled over, put your hands on the steering wheel and wait for the officer to approach the car. Unless your hands are on the wheel, an officer may believe you have a gun or another weapon. If a police officer asks for your license, insurance, or registration, let him or her know where they are. "OK, officer, I need to reach in my pocket for the license and the glove box for the insurance and registration." Provide the officer with every courtesy; they have a tough job to do.

As you go through corporate life, stay positive. Focus on the task at hand. Stay in the flow. Never stop learning. A healthy diet, along with a daily exercise regimen, will improve your overall well-being. Avoid eating desserts laden with sugar late at night. During the middle of the night, you'll keep waking up as your stomach digests what nutritionists refer to as a "sugar bomb." By taking good care of your body, you'll live longer. Plus, you'll have more energy during the day.

Work hard. Have fun. Add value.

Life is short, so maximize the ride.

THE END

CORPORATE RESOURCE GUIDE

What to tip a waiter, wine steward, concierge, or taxi driver is subjective. If you believe someone performed an excellent job, tip more. If someone did an average job, tip the minimum. Use the following chart, sourced from personal experiences, as a guide.

CATERER*

Delivery Fee — Typically $20, which often goes to pay for the catering truck
Preparers — $10 per person
Servers — $10 per person
Bartender — $20-$40 per person
* Check the bill; the caterer may include tips. If not, the more guests at your party, the higher the tips. Do not give all of the tips to one person and trust him or her to distribute it based on your wishes. Provide each tip individually (use small envelopes).

PERSONAL

Hairdresser — 15 percent to 20 percent of bill
Shampoo Person — $2 minimum
Barber — 15 percent to 20 percent of bill, or $2 minimum
Manicurist — 15 percent of bill
Spa/Salon — 15 percent to 20 percent of bill
Pizza Delivery — $2 per pizza (more in bad weather)
Food Delivery — 5 percent to 10 percent of bill (more in bad weather)
Grocery Loader — $1 to $3 (more if multiple bags)

HOTEL/TRAIN/CRUISE SHIP/STADIUM/TRAVEL

Bellhop — $1 per bag brought to a room ($2 minimum if one bag)
Doorman — $1 if they help with luggage, $1 if they hail a cab
Skycap — $1 per bag at curbside check-in, $2 if they carry it inside
Concierge — $5-$20 for reservations or tickets, more for great seats
Front Desk Clerk — $20-$40 based on room upgrade
Maid/Housekeeper — $2 to $5 per day
Stadium Usher — $1 per seat (wiped down)
Stadium Waiter — 15 percent to 20 percent of the food bill, 50 cents for a soft drink, $1 for alcoholic beverages
Taxi Driver — 15 percent of the fare, $1 per bag for assistance
Executive Sedan Driver — 15 percent to 20 percent of the fare, higher for bag assistance
Limousine Driver — 15 percent to 20 percent of the fare, higher for bag assistance or help with meeting items/equipment

BARS/RESTAURANTS

Waiter — 15 percent to 20 percent of the bill, excluding taxes (you can go with 10 percent if the service or food is bad)
Bartender — 15 percent to 20 percent of the bill, or 50 cents for a soft drink, $1 for alcoholic beverages
Headwaiter/Captain — Often shares tips with the waiter, or tip separately
Wine Steward/Sommelier — 15 percent of bottle cost
Coat Check — $1 per coat
Parking Valet/Garage Attendant — $2 for bringing the car
Lavatory Attendant — 50 cents to $1 per visit (stocked counter)

GOLF COURSE

Caddie — 50 percent of the caddie fee, food and beverage at turn
Forecaddie — A foursome should tip $50-$100 total
Caddie Master — 20 percent of the caddie fee if they provide a good caddie
Starter — No tip unless they did yeoman's work squeezing you in ($5-$10)
Bag Drop Attendees — $2-$3 per bag
Cart Return Attendees — $2-$5 per bag (if you don't have a caddie and they clean the clubs)
Beverage Cart — $1 tip per beverage, per stop

ALCOHOL PERCENTAGE BY VOLUME

If you plan to drive home, one or two drinks is the maximum you should consume over the course of an evening. Be sure to eat a meal and drink plenty of water. If you plan to drink more, use a designated driver or call a cab. In some areas, there are car services that offer one car and two drivers — one to drive you home, another to follow in your car. As a general rule, beer has the lowest alcohol percentage by volume, followed by wine, and then spirits. Drink responsibly.

Beer
— 3 percent to 10 percent, check the label for precise information

Hard Cider
— 4 percent to 8 percent

Wine
— 4 percent to 7 percent for wine coolers
— 8 percent to 15 percent for wine, both red and white
— Fortified wines are typically higher, 15 percent to 22 percent

Spirits
— 15 percent to 98 percent
Source: *AlcoholContents.com*

FOREIGN CUSTOMS

Read up on a particular country and its customs, both for business and pleasure, before you visit. Typically, the customs are the same if you're attending a local cultural event, a foreign embassy in the United States, or a consulate's home. For travel, I recommend *Fodor's Travel Guides*. For customs, try *ExecutivePlanet.com*. A cultural group such as the Asian Pacific American Chamber of Commerce or the American Arab Chamber of Commerce can provide assistance, as well.

DOMESTIC SALARIES

If you're fortunate enough to make it big, a domestic staff is a necessity. Here are the salary ranges of domestic employees from *ButlerBureau.com*. For added information, consult the Domestic Estate Managers Association.

Butler (standard) — $60,000-$120,000
Butler (cooks and/or P.A. skills) — $70,000-$150,000
Houseman — $45,000-$70,000
Valet/Under Butler/Footman — $45,000-$70,000
Butler (formal, oversees small staff) — $80,000-$150,000
Butler (formal, oversees 4+ staff) — $90,000-$180,000

Head Butler (multiple residences) — $140,000-$250,000
Estate Manager — $80,000-$125,000
Estate Manager (multiple properties) — $100,000-$250,000
Domestic Couple (Houseman/Cook) — $70,000-$100,000
Domestic Couple (caretaking) — $40,000-$75,000
Domestic Couple (management) — $80,000-$150,000
Private Chef (one person) — $50,000-$80,000
Private Chef (oversees small staff) — $80,000-$150,000
Cook/Housekeeper — $40,000-$80,000
Personal Assistant (office duties) — $60,000-$120,000
Personal Secretary — $60,000-$150,000

JOB INTERVIEWS KEYWORD: INTERVIEW1

EMPLOYERS:

◈ Make sure the office is neat and tidy.

◈ Does the recruit look you in the eye, or turn away? If a candidate can't maintain eye contact, he or she may have self-esteem issues.

◈ Check the resume carefully. Are there time gaps? If so, inquire why. Make sure to conduct a thorough background check. Ask for references, and check with them. Ask the reference about the candidate's work ethic, social skills, talents, and shortcomings (if any).

◈ Ask the candidate to tell an interesting story about his or her life. See how they respond and gauge their answer.

◈ Trust your instincts. Watch the candidate's mannerisms very closely. Do they keep looking around or are they focused on your questions?

◈ Give your undivided attention; you asked for the interview, after all. If a qualified candidate isn't comfortable, they'll likely look elsewhere. Be sure to offer a candidate something to drink.

◈ Did the candidate arrive with extra resumes to hand out? If so, it's a good sign he or she is prepared for the unexpected.

◈ If the candidate keeps looking at his or her smart phone or, worse, answers a text or call during the interview, it's probably best to move on (unless it truly is an emergency). If they can't nail an interview, there likely will be other problems down the road.

JOB CANDIDATES:

◉ Before you arrive for the interview, research the company, the prospective job, and the interviewer as best as possible. Talk to anyone you know who worked with the company, whether directly or as a vendor, supplier, or former employee.

◉ Practice your responses to standard questions such as why you're the best candidate for the job (don't brag). Don't lie on your resume.

◉ Dress professionally, which means a black or dark blue suit, white shirt, conservative tie, and matching, polished shoes. For ladies, a conservative business suit or dress is appropriate. You want to land the job because of your talents, not your looks. Wear accessories sparingly. You don't want to give the impression that you don't need the job or have self-esteem issues.

◉ Arrive a few minutes before the meeting. Allow plenty of travel time, and factor in rush hour. You don't want to be late. The prospective employer will consider it poor form if you are late (unless there's an accident or major storm). Study traffic patterns and consider a dry run.

◉ If you arrive early, grab a cup of coffee or a soda nearby. Don't drink too much caffeine. Your hands may be shaking already. If you feel a hot spell coming on, or you tend to sweat a lot, wear a light suit. Be sure to have a handkerchief.

◉ After checking in with the receptionist, stay active while waiting. Don't sit there staring blindly into space. If you make a call, be prepared to hang up right away when the interviewer arrives. To stay busy, review the company again on your smart phone, tablet, or laptop. Look for any late-breaking news and comment on it during the interview.

◉ When the interviewer arrives, stand up right away, introduce yourself, shake their hand firmly, and make eye contact. When you walk to the office or conference room for the interview, stay in stride with the interviewer. Don't walk in front of or behind the interviewer. If an assistant arrives to escort you to the meeting, be courteous and strike up a pleasant conversation.

◉ Once the interview starts, thank the interviewer for his or her time and consideration. Concentrate on their mannerisms, what they're wearing, and how they speak, and be sure to make private observations about the room. Is everything well-organized, or are things messy and strewn here and there? A sloppy office may mean the company is short-staffed. You may be required to do more work than advertised.

◉ Answer all questions as best as possible. Do not read from notes. Make sure you ask questions. What work is required, what are the salary and benefits, what are the hours, etc.?

⦿ When the interview is over, ask about the next steps. Thank the interviewer for his or her time, give a firm handshake, and make eye contact again. Be sure to push your chair back to its original space. If you accepted a water or coffee, take it with you, or ask for the location of the nearest trash receptacle.

⦿ If possible, check out the restrooms. Again, are they neat or untidy? This often speaks volumes about the company you're about to work with.

⦿ Be sure to follow up as prescribed.

⦿ At times, you may be the odd candidate out, or the company is using you to fill a certain requirement. For example, a company may have a policy of interviewing three different people for every job opening. The employer may have a preferred candidate, and he or she is just going through the motions by bringing you in for an interview. Hopefully, your research will pick up on this. The interview can't hurt and, who knows, you may land a position down the road.

⦿ To make a lasting impression, you could create a video or a social media campaign about why you're the best candidate for the job. Make sure it's original, compelling, and won't hurt your chances (some companies don't want it known that they're hiring). Be sure to test the video or social campaign among a few family members and friends before releasing it live or providing it to the employer.

⦿ If you're switching from one employer to another, keep everything confidential. Make sure the new job is yours before giving your two-week notice. If possible, allow your current employer the opportunity to make a counter-offer. If they decline, take the new job.

⦿ Keep your head high. Don't trash your former employer. You may be working with them two or three years down the road, or you could become a supplier or vendor. You never know what the future holds, so be courteous, watch your back, be prepared to defend yourself or a colleague, and do the best job you can. People like, and will reward, a hard worker. Soak up as much knowledge as you can.

Formal Place Setting in the United States

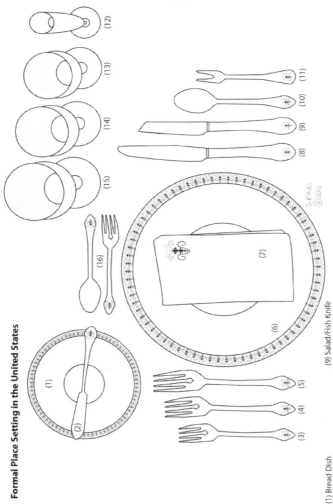

(1) Bread Dish
(2) Butter Knife
(3) Fish Fork
(4) Salad Fork
(5) Dinner Fork
(6) Charger (other dishes will top this)
(7) Napkin (place in lap right away)
(8) Dinner Knife

(9) Salad/Fish Knife
(10) Soup Spoon
(11) Shellfish Fork
(12) Champagne Flute
(13) White Wine Glass
(14) Red Wine Glass
(15) Water Glass
(16) Dessert Fork/Spoon

In Europe, the position of the salad fork and dinner fork will be reversed, given Europeans prefer to have their salad served after the main course.

Design by Stephanie King

ABOUT THE TEAM

JOSEF BASTIAN, Writing Consultant

Josef Bastian is a thought leader who, since 1991, has specialized in broad-based work force development, education, and training initiatives. An internationally published author and poet, Bastian's works include *Nain Rouge, A Pardon for Vincent, Somewhere in Middle America, Next Halloween, Beyond the Little Brauhaus, Big Boss Man, Keith Doodle Saves Christmas, Middleness,* and *A Day in the Life of Denver Penny.*

Bastian holds advanced degrees in instructional design and learning technology from Oakland University in Rochester Hills and the University of Detroit Mercy, both in Michigan, and Oxford University in England. He can be reached at *jbastian67@msn.com.*

CASSIDY ZOBL, Designer

Cassidy Zobl is an award-winning graphic designer and art director. Since 2007, she has served as art director of *Hour Detroit,* a successful lifestyle magazine that serves more than 46,000 monthly readers in metro Detroit. In addition, she has created multimedia marketing campaigns, program books, playbills, posters, signage, logos, and promotional material for a diverse roster of private businesses and individuals.

Since joining Hour Media as an advertising designer in 2005, Zobl has been honored with multiple gold and silver medals, including best feature design in *FOLIO* magazine's national competition (2011), feature spread design by the Society of Professional Journalists (2010), and the General Excellence category from the City and Regional Magazine Association (2009), the organization's top award. She also won an Ozzie for "Best Use of Photography" for a fashion feature (2012). For more information, visit *cassidyzobl.com, after-six-design.com,* or e-mail *cassidyz@gmail.com.*

ANNE BERRY DAUGHERTY, Copy Editor

Anne Berry Daugherty received a Bachelor of Arts degree in advertising from Michigan State University in East Lansing. She has worked as a writer and editor for Sandy Corp., The Quarton Group, and Crain Communications. She is currently a freelance copy editor with a variety of clients in metro Detroit, including the Community Foundation for Southeast Michigan. She also does work for publications such as *DBusiness* magazine, *Hour Detroit* magazine, *Carolinas Golf,* the *Metropolitan Detroit Menu Guide,* and the *Metropolitan Detroit Guest and Resource Guide.* She can be reached at *jd2794@aol.com.*

ABOUT THE AUTHOR

 For more than 20 years, R.J. King has covered one of the nation's busiest news towns. He has generated award-winning coverage as editor and co-founder of *DBusiness* magazine and as a business writer at *The Detroit News*. Mr. King has written more than 4,000 articles and interviewed hundreds of business owners, CEOs, entrepreneurs, scholars, artists, and politicians. He also attends 200-plus corporate and charitable events annually, including the North American International Auto Show, shareholder meetings, industry conferences, cultural ceremonies, and charitable fundraisers.

Mr. King is a member of the board of directors of Beyond Basics, the Asian Pacific American Chamber of Commerce, Detroit Athletic Club Executives Club, Detroit Aircraft Corp., and the Brother Rice Business Alliance. He also serves on the Board of Trustees of The Parade Co.

DBusiness, launched in 2006, garnered nine editorial gold and silver medals from the Alliance of Area Business Publications (2010-11), including being named the top business magazine among 70 regional business publications in the United States, Canada, Puerto Rico, and Australia, which collectively reach more than 1.2 million professionals. Over the course of 16 years at *The Detroit News*, Mr. King traveled in Europe and Asia, where he covered international business and political leaders. While back home, he broke hundreds of stories such as Ford Motor Co.'s $2-billion transformation of the historic Rouge Industrial Complex in Dearborn, Michigan into a model of sustainable manufacturing.

Mr. King grew up in Bloomfield Village, a suburb of Detroit, where he was the middle child — three older sisters and a brother, and three younger sisters and a brother. As a middle child, Mr. King learned to negotiate positive outcomes at a young age. An alumnus of the University of Michigan-Dearborn, Mr. King lives in a historic neighborhood in Detroit.

For inquiries: *rjking@rjkingpublishing.com*

Made in the USA
Lexington, KY
25 June 2013